# TACO OBSESSION

# TACO
# OBSESSION

## Essential Recipes to Celebrate the Flavors of Mexico

ADRIANA MARTIN

R

ROCKRIDGE
PRESS

For general information on our other products and services, please contact our Customer Care Department within the United States at (866) 744-2665, or outside the United States at (510) 253-0500.

Paperback ISBN: 978-1-63807-461-8
eBook ISBN: 978-1-63807-249-2

Manufactured in the United States of America

Interior and Cover Designer: Angela Navarra
Art Producer: Sara Feinsten
Editor: Sierra Machado
Production Editor: Caroline Flanagan
Production Manager: Holly Haydash

Photography © 2022 Darren Muir with food styling by Yolanda Muir, except pp. 15; all other imagery used under license from shutterstock.com.

10 9 8 7 6 5 4 3 2 1 0

I dedicate this cookbook to my family, friends, and all those food lovers obsessed with tacos and authentic Mexican street food. So, let's eat some tacos!

# CONTENTS

# INTRODUCTION

**Let's face it, who *isn't* obsessed with tacos?** If there is a person out there who hasn't yet fallen in love with the flavors of homemade Mexican food and real-deal tacos, I have not met them. I am so excited to have the opportunity to share with you what I know about tacos and authentic Mexican street food.

Tacos are the quintessential street food. But how did the taco tradition start? The etymology of the word *taco* is debated, but it likely comes from the Nahuatl *tlahco*, which means "half" or "in the middle" because the stuffing goes in the center of the tortilla. However, some historians think the name comes from *tacualli*, "a stuffed tortilla with stew."

In Mexican cuisine, tacos are made with anything. You can make tacos with *guisados* (meat and vegetable stews used as taco fillings), grilled meats, vegetables, beans, and rice. Or they can even come in the form of a fresh rolled tortilla with salt or with nothing but salsa, called *tacos de aire*.

My connection with tacos is deep. I am Mexican, and tacos are part of my culture, so I grew up eating tacos. My mom was resourceful. She transformed leftovers into tacos that everyone enjoyed. Yes, tacos are all about the leftovers! As a young adult attending university, tacos were my go-to quick but satisfying meal. Local taquerías in Mexico City became important hangouts to eat and socialize with friends. In Mexico, the after-party happens at the taquería, which is why taquería restaurants stay open until sunrise.

The taco culture is ingrained in the Mexican culinary culture. For generations, tacos have been considered food for the working class due to their portability and low cost. In the old days, tacos were the conduit for women to support their families. And that is how the *tacos de canasta* originated in 1950 in Tlaxcala. These tacos have simple ingredients, such as potato mash with chorizo and picadillo. The tacos are kept warm by a steaming

technique with hot oil wrapped inside a big plastic bag covered with a tablecloth and stored inside a canasta or basket. Some also called them *tacos sudados, de olla,* or steamed tacos. To this day, this kind of street food is prevalent in Mexico City.

With the Mexican migration to the United States, the taco culture transcended frontiers and became an obvious choice for fast-food stardom because tacos are adaptable to any ingredients and easy to make.

Mexico's pride and joy have gone international. Nowadays, tacos are served everywhere. Many chefs have used the Mexican taco concept to create other tacos by using Korean, American barbeque, or Mediterranean flavors, which have resulted in the new trend for fusion tacos.

This cookbook aims to keep the recipes as authentic as possible. With that said, some recipes are labor-intensive, will require a pressure cooker or a Dutch oven, and can include ingredients that might call for a visit to the Mexican supermarket or online shopping at a specialty store. Rest assured, I will be providing expert tips and tricks to make the cooking process as easy as possible while keeping the authenticity of the dishes for a true Mexican taco experience.

Each region in Mexico has its own taco staple. Chapter 1 provides details on the most popular tacos by region and the culinary diversity illustrated with a map for easy identification. This book includes a variety of recipes suitable for breakfast, lunch, and dinner and favorite Mexican staples, such as salsas, side dishes, delightful desserts, classic cocktails, and *aguas frescas.*

I hope you get a lot out of this book—but mainly many great tacos to get you inspired to cook.

## CHAPTER 1

# FOR THE LOVE OF TACOS

**T**his chapter is all about the history and evolution of tacos. Since tortillas are the main ingredient for tacos, I provide information on the different tortilla options and comparisons.

I also include details on regional tastes for tacos, such as the top-ten most popular tacos in Mexico. You'll also find in-depth information on ingredients and must-have kitchen tools when making tacos at home. Tacos pair well with a beverage, so I've also included insights about classic Mexican drinks.

# A BRIEF HISTORY

The *taquera* (taco) culture as we know it today started in Mexico City, but there is no certainty when tacos were invented. Historians believe tacos first appeared in Mexico during the pre-Hispanic times, long before the conquest in 1521, when the Aztec empire fell and Hernán Cortés, a Spanish conquistador, claimed Mexico for Spain. This is one of the primary events in the Spanish colonization of the Americas. Those first tacos came stuffed with chile peppers, squash, cactus, and other humble ingredients. The first taco record appeared in Manuel Payno's novel *Bandits of the Cold River*, published in 1891. The first time the word *taco* was officially accepted was in the *Dictionary of Mexicanisms* of Feliz Ramos I. Duarte, published in 1895.

## Origins in Mexico

The name taco likely comes from the Nahuatl *tlahco*, which means half or in the middle because the stuffing goes in the center of the tortilla. Some historians think the name comes from *tacuallivy* or a stuffed tortilla with stew.

Historians also mention that the first famous tacos were called *tacos mineros* because of their association with the Mexican silver mines. These "tacos" were not food. The so-called tacos were filled with gunpowder, wrapped with paper sheets, and placed in the rock to extract the precious metal. However, tacos are inexpensive to feed the crowds; thus, miners are fed with tacos mineros, or Pork and Beans Miner Tacos (page 73). These are a staple in the mining states of Guanajuato, Hidalgo, and Zacatecas.

As time passed and the conquest occurred, tacos continued being a part of everyday life. During the Mexican Revolution (November 20, 1910, to May 21, 1920), tacos cooked by Las Soldaderas fed the rebels because one guisado could make many tacos. Soon tacos became a staple of the working class due to their portability and affordability.

In the 1930s and 1940s, women became breadwinners. An easy way to generate income was selling tacos, providing a service to those late-night blue-collar workers or early risers needing to grab an inexpensive bite before or after work. This is when informal taquería stands started to appear. Offal (organ meats) taco offerings were abundant and everyday items were on the menu.

By the 1970s, tacos started being embraced by the upper classes, and formal taquerías with extensive grilling in open kitchens appeared in high-end communities where *tacos al carbon*, or beef cooked on charcoal grills, became instant favorites using better meat cuts.

## Rise in America

The taco arrived in America in the early 1900s with the Mexican immigrants that worked on the railroads. By the 1920s, tacos were pretty famous, and that is when tacos were Americanized, using local ingredients and adding yellow cheese and sour cream garnished with lettuce and chopped tomatoes. In the 1950s, Glen Bell, the founder of Taco Bell, introduced tacos to America as fast food. California's crispy taco and Texas's puffy taco have become culinary heavens for taco lovers.

## Present Day

The taco culture has come a long way since it started. The taco became trendy after being elevated by fusion cuisine. An example of this trend is the famous Korean tacos attributed to Mark Manguera and Roy Choi of Kogi Korean BBQ, a taco truck. The idea was inspired by Beef Asada Tacos (page 71) and Korean cuisine.

Classic Birria Tacos (page 66) became a social media phenomenon in the United States, but they originally started in Jalisco, the home of authentic birria. These tacos consist of braised meat stuffed in a fried taco with cheese and are served alongside the braising broth for dipping. Tacos are beloved worldwide, and in America, a whopping 4.5 billion tacos are eaten per year. There's National Taco Day (October 4th) and Taco Tuesdays!

# TACOS BY REGION

The culinary diversity in Mexico is vast. Each state has its food staples and tacos staples as well. The map on the next page shows a few of the most loved tacos in Mexico and the region where they come from, but by no means does this map show an exhaustive list of all the options Mexicans love.

Each area embraces its local ingredients, reflected in the guisados and tacos being consumed. In the north and the Pacific, you'll notice that beef, seafood, dairy, and game are prevalent. In the gulf and the south, the most traditional cooking methods are used to create afro-inspired dishes with banana leaves and tropical ingredients, and an earth oven cooking called *pib*.

Central Mexico is where the Spanish colony was based. Thus, many dishes are a fusion of European Spanish food mixed with local ingredients and a new invention (sometimes attributed to nuns in Puebla): mole poblano.

## The 10 Most Popular Tacos in Mexico

**Tacos al pastor** (Mexico City)

**Tacos de carnitas** (Michoacán)

**Tacos de carne asada** (Coahuila, Nuevo Leon, Mexico City)

**Tacos de cochinita pibil** (Yucatan)

**Tacos de dorados** (San Luis Potosí, Sinaloa)

**Tacos de langosta** (Baja California Norte)

**Tacos de guisado o acorazados** (Morelos, Mexico City, Puebla)

**Tacos de barbacoa** (Hidalgo, Chihuahua, Durango)

**Tacos campechanos** (Querétaro, San Luis Potosí, Mexico City)

**Tacos envenenados** (Zacatecas)

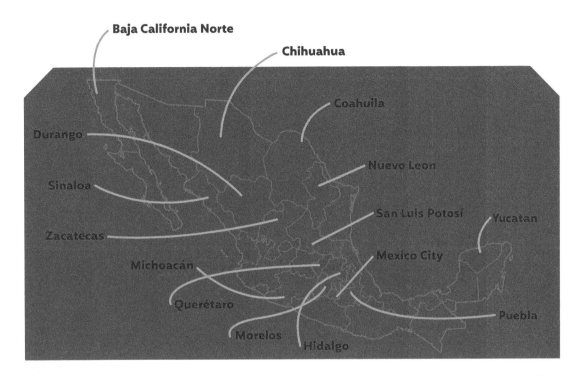

**Baja California Norte**

**Chihuahua**

Coahuila

Durango

Nuevo Leon

Sinaloa

San Luis Potosí

Yucatan

Zacatecas

Mexico City

Michoacán

Querétaro

Puebla

Morelos

Hidalgo

**Tacos al pastor:** These tacos appeared in the 1920s when Lebanese immigrants arrived in Mexico. With them, they brought the shawarma, which consisted of thin slices of pre-marinated lamb meat stacked and roasted slowly on a vertical grill. Since lamb was scarce and expensive, pork became a meat replacement, which is how tacos al pastor came about. The base for the marinade includes dried peppers, achiote, vinegar, citrus juices, and Mexican spices. In the north, these tacos are called *tacos de trompo* and are typically served with chopped onions, pineapple, and cilantro and garnished with taquera salsa and lime juice.

**Tacos de carnitas:** The first pork carnitas feast occurred right after the conquest. Pork was not a protein consumed by the Aztecs, as it didn't exist as an option for them until the Spaniards arrived in the New World. The addition of pork to the diet transformed Mexican cuisine into what it is today. The pork cooks in copper pots for hours until the meat becomes tender and the skin browns. The garnishes include onions, cilantro, and salsa verde. The most famous carnitas are from Michoacán.

**Tacos de carne asada:** Beef grilled tacos originate in the North of Mexico, where *parrilladas,* or informal outdoor cookouts, rule. It is common to marinate *bistecs* (think steaks) with beer and spices. These tacos are famous in many northern states, but the name and the garnishes differ. For example, in Monterrey, these tacos are called *tacos de arrachera.* In Chihuahua, these tacos come wrapped in flour tortillas and with a side of grilled onions. In Mexico City, they're called *tacos al carbon* because the beef cooks on a charcoal grill. The beef is chopped and garnished with onions, cilantro, and lime wedges, and drizzled with salsa verde or roja.

**Tacos de cochinita pibil:** The pork *pibil* tacos are typical Yucatán dishes whose tradition dates back to pre-Hispanic times. Classic *cochinita*, shredded pork pibil from Yucatán, uses an annatto paste marinade with citrus and spices and is then cooked wrapped in banana leaves inside a Mayan pib (oven made with dirt and covered with hot stones). The cooked meat is shredded and served inside warm corn tortillas topped with pickled onions and habanero salsa. Although these tacos are especially famous in Yucatán and Campeche, they are prepared and enjoyed nationwide.

**Tacos dorados:** The crispy fried tacos originated in Sinaloa and San Luis Potosí. In Mexico City, fried taquitos are called *flautas* when rolled tightly—typically served drenched in guacamole sauce, lettuce, and Mexican crema. They can come folded or rolled, and the stuffing is a combination of potato mash and cheese with shredded beef, chicken, beans, or shrimp. In Chihuahua, fried tacos come stuffed with beef picadillo and are served with generous amounts of shredded raw carrots, beets, lettuce or cabbage, and hot sauce. Crispy *taquitos de papa* are paired with a spicy tomato broth in other parts of Mexico.

**Tacos de langosta:** Lobster tacos are a favorite dish served in El Rosarito, a coastal beach town located in the Baja California area south of the border with Mexico. These tacos have become a favorite in the region and are highly rated by tourists. When serving lobster tacos, one of the staples is adding a small bowl of refried beans and rice and a chile de árbol hot sauce. Lobster tacos are served in a warm flour tortilla.

**Tacos de guisado o acorazados:** This type of taco was born in Cuautla, Morelos, in 1908. These tacos were popular street food sold by mothers looking to generate income. Later, *tacos acorazados*, or stew tacos, became a staple in Cuernavaca. Currently, stew tacos can be found almost anywhere in Mexico because it is a great way to feed many with one guisado or provide a variety of flavors by making several options. The most popular guisados are *chicharron en salsa*, chorizo potato, *rajas con crema*, chicken mole, tinga, *carne en su jugo*, refried beans, and carne à la Mexicana.

**Tacos de barbacoa:** Some say these tacos started in San Luis Potosí, where barbacoa is made with *borrego* (lamb), *chivo* (goat), or beef. But these tacos are famous in Hidalgo, State of Mexico, Tlaxcala, and DF (Distrito Federal). In the north, barbacoa is also popular in Durango, and in Monterrey it is made with *cabrito* (young goat). Typical barbacoa is made with goat or lamb and is oven cooked. The cooking process is lengthy, and many use firewood for a more authentic barbacoa experience. The tradition is to eat these tacos on Sunday paired with lamb consommé, salsa de chile de árbol, and limes.

**Tacos campechanos:** These tacos are famous in Querétaro and have a mix of lean and fatty meats. These tacos can include chicharrones, chorizo (longaniza), or bacon combined with shredded beef, pork, or chicken. These are the best way to create a taco meal using leftovers.

**Tacos envenenados:** The urban legend says these tacos were made famous by Don Lauro, a taquería owner in Zacatecas. He promoted his tacos, saying, "If you want to get poisoned, eat tacos." From that moment, the tacos were called poisoned tacos. These tacos mix spicy potatoes with chorizo and refried pinto beans and are folded and fried.

# THE INGREDIENTS

These are the main ingredients used in this book's recipes. Many of these you will know well, but others you may not be familiar with. Don't be afraid to try something new—that's part of the fun!

**Achiote paste:** Achiote, or annatto, is used for coloring and seasoning. It comes in a paste, powdered, or square. This condiment is a main ingredient for cochinita pibil and tacos al pastor.

**Beans:** There are over seventy native bean species cultivated in Mexico. The most common are pinto, mayo, and black beans. All are cooked in a traditional clay pot (*frijoles de olla*) or using an Instant Pot. Canned options could work, but there is nothing better than homemade.

**Chorizo:** The most common form of this sausage is from Sinaloa and Sonora. It has ground pork meat mixed with high-fat cuts. It crumbles when cooked. The flavor is spicy with smoky tones due to the chile guajillo, vinegar, and spices.

**Dried and fresh peppers:** Here are the main peppers we'll work with for spicing up our tacos!

> **Chile de árbol:** This chile is six times hotter than a jalapeño, between 15,000 and 30,000 Scoville Heat Units. The peppers come fresh and dried and are the main ingredient for taquera salsa and vinegar-based hot sauces.

> **Chile guajillo:** This dried pepper comes in two sizes: one is puya, and the standard size is guajillo—both are used for sauces, birria, and spicy broths. The flavor is mild and smoky, and the heat level range is between 2,500 to 5,000 on the Scoville scale.

> **Chipotle peppers:** These peppers are dried jalapeños smoked for added flavor and used in sauces and dishes such as tinga. The heat level ranges from 2,500 to 8,000 Scoville Heat Units. Chipotles are also known as meco and morita.

**Jalapeño and serrano peppers:** Typically used raw for chopped salsa, guacamole, and cooked sauces with tomatoes or tomatillos. These peppers are also popular for pickling mixed with carrots. Jalapeños are mildly hot, averaging around 5,000 Scoville Heat Units. In comparison, serrano peppers can go up to 15,000 Scoville Heat Units.

**Masa harina:** Masa harina is coarse white or blue corn flour used for making tortillas. The familiar brands are Maseca or Masabrosa and both work for making masa for tortillas.

**Mole:** Mole comes in a paste ready to use. It has a mix of dried chiles, nuts, Mexican chocolate, and spices. Recommend either Oaxacan-style (mole negro) or poblano.

**Onion, garlic, cilantro, and limes:** These four ingredients are indispensable in authentic Mexican cooking. Use onions and garlic raw or roasted for preparing salsas and guisados. Cilantro is the perfect garnish for tacos and salsas for an herbaceous touch. Limes are used most often for marinades and drinks.

**Rice:** Long-grain rice for cooking Mexican-style rice is recommended. Rice also makes horchata and Mexican Rice Pudding (page 113). Choose a Latino brand if possible, as it's more authentic in flavor and aroma than other brands.

**Spices and seeds:** Cumin, marjoram, bay leaves, allspice, cinnamon, cloves, and black pepper are everyday seasonings for pork, fish, and other meats. They are also used for pickling and making sauces and desserts. The pepitas, peanuts, and sesame seeds are for salsas and moles, add texture, or are used as a garnish.

**Tomatillos:** Tomatillos are Mexican husk tomatoes, but they are related to gooseberries. The flavor is acidic, and they can be green or deep purple. They are essential for salsa verde.

**Tomatoes:** Tomatoes are vital in Mexican cuisine for making sauces, pico de gallo, and guacamole, among many other dishes. Roma tomatoes are the most common and appropriate for boiling and roasting. The juicier beefsteak tomatoes are preferred for salsas.

**Queso cotija:** This cheese originated in Michoacán. Made with raw milk and covered in a peppery red sauce, it is matured for three months. It has a robust, salty taste with a refined aroma. The cheese crumbles serve as topping for tacos dorados and other Mexican dishes.

# TORTILLAS

The origin of the Mexican corn tortilla dates from 500 BCE. The Mayan sacred book, the *Popol Vuh*, describes how the gods used corn masa to create the civilization. The Mesoamerican cultures, which include Zapotec, Mixtec, Mexica or Aztec, and Nahua, all contributed to Mexico's culinary culture as we know it today, and tortillas are a big part of their legacy. Tortillas were called *tlaxcalli* and made with nixtamalized corn. Nixtamalization is a traditional cooking process that neutralizes the corn grain acidity using food-grade lime and water, making the corn softer. When ground, it turns into masa harina, which, when added to water, turns into masa for tortillas. In the old days, the grinding of the corn and the crafting of the tortillas was done by hand. But this practice changed in 1947 when Fausto Celorio Mendoza invented the first tortilla machine prototype, and grinding companies started processing and commercializing the nixtamal corn. This was when the *tortilladora* automation concept came about. Nowadays, thousands of tortilla factories around Mexico still use this machinery to make massive amounts of corn tortillas daily.

## CORN VS. FLOUR

Corn tortillas are made with masa harina, water, and salt. In comparison, flour tortillas are made with wheat flour, lard, water, and salt. Corn tortillas appeared first, as corn was the base of the diet before the conquest. The Spaniards brought wheat and flat-breads, which later became flour tortillas. Corn tortillas are widespread in Mexico, but flour tortillas are standard in the North and have different shapes and sizes. Chihuahua is known for its thick and small flour tortillas. And Sonora is known for paper-thin ultra-large tortillas called *sobaqueras*, which are perfect for burritos.

## HOMEMADE VS. STORE-BOUGHT

As my mom said, homemade is best. But if you do not have time, several brands make good-quality corn or flour tortillas suitable for tacos. Check how to make Red Corn Tortillas (page 88) or Homemade Flour Tortillas (page 101) in chapter 6.

### HARD VS. SOFT

Hard tortillas are called tostadas, or the American version is known as taco shells. The idea of taco shells was inspired by the Mexican tacos dorados. This humble dish was intended to last longer than a soft tortilla that would become soggy and not hold the meat or the guisado. Taco shells first appeared in the 1950s when tacos became fast food, thanks to Glen Bell, the creator of Taco Bell. Soft tortillas are the most common when making authentic tacos. If you're craving crispy tacos but want an authentic experience, I recommend making tacos dorados instead of using taco shells.

### HOW TO WARM

In a comal or nonstick skillet, heat your tortillas over medium heat for 30 to 45 seconds on each side, until soft and pliable, then transfer them to a platter, where they will wait to be filled.

### HOW TO STORE

If making fresh tortillas at home, preserve them wrapped in a cloth and inside a plastic bag. Corn and flour tortillas are freezer-friendly. I recommend using vacuum-seal bags, wrapping the tortillas in parchment paper, and freezing them for future use. Tortillas typically stay fresh for up to a month in the freezer.

# THE TOOLS

There are a few gadgets and utensils that will make your life easier and set you up for success when cooking Mexican tacos at home. Check what you have in your kitchen before investing in new cooking tools; you may already have many of these items handy. You'll be upping your game in Mexican cooking and authentic taco crafting with these tools.

**Cast-iron grilling pan:** Many Mexican tacos require grilled meats. We recommend having a cast-iron grilling pan without using an outdoor charcoal grill. The cast-iron grill provides the characteristic marks of carne asada and is perfect for tacos al pastor or grilling veggies and onions.

**Clay pot:** Mexican clay pots are not only pretty but cook wonderful *caldos* (broths) and beans, are perfect for braising, frying, and cooking rice, and can be used as a mixing bowl when preparing masa for tortillas. Clay pots are traditional and nontoxic. Make sure the bottom has an imprint noting that the pot is food safe. Cure the clay pot by rubbing a garlic clove on the inside and outside of the pot, filling it with water, turning the stove to medium heat, and cooking until the water reduces to one cup. Don't have a clay pot? Instead, use a cast-iron Dutch oven or a frying pan.

**Comal or cast-iron griddle:** A comal is a flat grill used for many purposes, not only for cooking tortillas. It is excellent for roasting peppers, tomatoes, and garlic for salsas. Use a nonstick skillet or a cast-iron griddle if you do not have a comal. See tortilla warming instructions using a comal on page 11.

**Electric pressure cooker/Instant Pot:** An electric pressure cooker saves time and helps achieve the best results when cooking meats, stews, and beans—having a pressure cooker helps when making Lean Carnitas Tacos (page 72), barbacoa, chicken for shredding, broths, and refried beans. I use a six-quart Instant Pot in these recipes, but feel free to use whatever brand of electric pressure cooker you have.

**Knives and chopping blocks:** A paring knife and a chef's knife come in handy as Mexican cuisine also includes lots of chopping and meat slicing and cutting. You will need one chopping block for produce and one for meats. Food safety is essential, and avoiding cross contamination is imperative.

**Molcajete:** The molcajete is a volcanic stone mortar used for mashing, grinding, and blending. It is recommended for making homemade Mexican salsas as it provides an authentic chunky texture. However, a blender or food processor could work, too.

**Tortilla press:** The heavy metal press is the perfect size for making medium-size corn tortillas for tacos. If you plan to make homemade tortillas, this is a recommended investment. A replacement could be a plate, a rolling pin, or your hands extending the dough and forming the tortilla using a plastic liner.

**Utensils:** Investing in a good set of cooking utensils is always a good idea. I like stainless steel because it is durable, food safe, and easy to clean. You will need a solid turner, a slotted turner or spoon, solid spoon, ladle, tongs, cheese grater, garlic crusher, can opener, peeler, whisk, and masher.

# ¡SALUD!

To create an authentic Mexican taco experience, drinks are in order. This book includes several alcoholic and nonalcoholic options, such as Piña Colada Agua Fresca (page 108), Mango-Lime Ague Fresca (page 109), and Oatmeal Horchata (page 110). Or, if you are more adventurous, try The Hidalgo (page 107) or a Mango Mezcal Mojito (page 106).

When considering a tequila or mezcal cocktail, consider that each has an entirely different flavor profile. Mezcal is a distilled spirit made from an agave plant called agave mezcalero. Tequila is a distilled spirit made only from the blue agave plant. It has a smoother, richer flavor when aged and labeled *reposado* or *añejo*. Tequila is a controlled denomination of origin that is internationally recognized. In contrast, mezcal has a smoky flavor with a rustic flair. And the denomination of origin is reserved for Zacatecas, Tamaulipas, Guanajuato, San Luis Potosí, Durango, Guerrero, Michoacán, and Oaxaca.

Popular drink origins are often disputed, but here are some likely roots of classic cocktails and spirits.

**Margarita:** Invented in 1938 by Carlos Herrera, a Tijuana restaurateur. The drink mixes citrus juice with triple sec and tequila blanco. It is served in a cup with a salted rim and ice.

 **Mezcal:** Made with oven-cooked agave mezcalero, it has a smoky flavor. The most famous mezcal is from Oaxaca, and its production is entirely handmade.

 **Michelada:** First served in the 1970s in a bar in San Luis Potosí. *Mi Chelada* is slang for "my cold beer." The beer is poured over ice and dressed with lime juice, salt, and Tabasco sauce.

 **Paloma:** Invented by Javier Delgado, the La Capillita bar owner in Jalisco in 1860. The beverage has grapefruit soda, tequila blanco, and ice, and it is garnished with lime and grapefruit slices.

 **Tequila:** An *aguardiente*, or strong alcoholic beverage, of ancestral origin. It has been produced since the sixteenth century in Tequila, Jalisco, and is made of distilled and aged agave azul juice.

# GLOSSARY

**Adobo:** A thick sauce made with dried chiles to season meats

**Alambre:** A skewer for making Mexican kebabs

**Asada:** Grilled; a common word for grilled beef tacos

**Caldo:** This word means broth. Some tacos pair with tomato- or dried-pepper-based broths. Examples include tacos dorados and birria.

**Chamoy:** A sweet-and-sour sauce made with apricots, vinegar, hibiscus flowers, dried chiles, and fruits, used for crafting beverages and candies

**De olla:** This expression is used when steaming tacos or cooking beans in a clay pot.

**Escabeche:** Pickling

**Flor de calabaza:** Zucchini blossom

**Guisados:** These are meat and vegetable dishes cooked in a sauce with chili peppers, tomatoes, spices, and aromatic herbs. The guisado is used as a stuffing for tacos.

**Masa:** Dough for corn tortillas

**Molcajetear:** Using the molcajete (stone mortar) to grind spices and craft chunky salsas

**Parrilla or parrillada:** A grill or a gathering involving a group getting together and grilling

**Picadillo:** Ground meat cooked with vegetables, Mexican spices, and tomato sauce

**Queso fundido:** Melted cheese on a charcoal grill

**Salsa taquera or salsa cruda:** Taquera means hot sauce for tacos, and cruda means a hot sauce made with raw produce such as salsa verde with tomatillo.

**Taquiza:** A taco party

**Tinga:** The Spanish word for a stew or guisado

**Tortear:** The action of making corn tortillas with your hands

**Tortilladora:** A metal tortilla press

**Trompo:** This is a standing grill used for making pastor tacos.

# THE NEW TACO FRONTIER

Tacos have evolved throughout history and are currently one of the most representative icons of Mexican cuisine. The first mentions in Mexican culinary history say that Moctezuma used tortillas to hold his food, forming something like a taco; the second was when women prepared lunch baskets for workingmen, including guisados wrapped in tortillas.

Over the centuries, the most famous tacos in Mexico emerged in 1908 in Cuautla, Morelos. In 1950 the tacos de canasta appeared in San Vicente Xiloxochitla. Still, it was not until 1966 that the king of tacos, inspired by the Arab shawarma, the taco al pastor, was first served at the taquería El Tizoncito.

In 2017, the extravagant Golden Taco was born in Los Cabos thanks to chef Juan Licerio Alcalá, who made a taco with Kobe beef, langoustine, Beluga caviar, and black truffle Brie cheese—wrapped on a homemade corn tortilla and twenty-four-karat gold foil.

When thinking about tacos, we must consider all the transformations they have undergone over the years to become the ones we know today. Although we have the idea that a taco must be made a certain way, the truth is that the magic of this dish is precisely that possibility of adapting to any cuisine and any taste.

That is why taco fusions such as tacos Árabes, Korean tacos, Tex-Mex puffy tacos, and kosher tacos work so well and have become a trend. If you are a taco lover, try mixing your favorite flavors and making them into a taco. You'll be surprised by the results. Anything can go inside a corn or flour tortilla.

Tacos are not only easy to make, but they can satisfy the most demanding palates. Maybe that is the reason they are such a beloved food worldwide. Anywhere you go, there is a taco awaiting you.

## CHAPTER 2

# EGGS AND VEGETABLES

< Mexican Egg Scramble Tacos, page 24

# SQUASH BLOSSOM TACOS
## *Tacos de Flor de Calabaza*

Flowers inside a taco? The flores de calabaza are a delicacy and have existed since pre-Hispanic times. You'll most often find zucchini flowers in salads, quesadillas, soups, or stuffed with cheese and fried in a light, airy batter. The flavor is subtle, and they are easy to cook. You'll love to eat them inside a taco sautéed à la Mexicana with garnishes.

2 tablespoons corn oil

½ medium onion, finely chopped

1 or 2 serrano chiles, seeded and finely chopped

2 medium tomatoes, chopped

Salt

1 pound squash blossoms, stemmed, stamens removed, and chopped

12 (6-inch) corn tortillas, warmed

**GARNISHES**

1 cup crumbled queso fresco

½ cup Raw Green Salsa (page 94)

½ cup Mexican crema

1. In a medium sauté pan or skillet, heat the oil over medium-high heat and sauté the onion and chiles, occasionally stirring, for 2 to 3 minutes, until the onion turns translucent.

2. Add the tomatoes and sauté for 2 minutes. Season with salt to taste. Add the squash blossoms and sauté just until they start to wilt. Remove from the heat.

3. Spoon 3 tablespoons of the filling into the middle of each warmed tortilla and fold. Garnish the tacos with queso fresco, salsa, and Mexican crema.

4. Store leftover cooked squash blossoms in an airtight container in the refrigerator for up to 2 days.

**TIP:** You can usually find zucchini blossoms at your local farmers' market. They should be firm and free of any bruising. Fresh zucchini flowers are only available during the fall (September to October), so buy canned when not in season. Or replace the zucchini blossoms with corn and zucchini.

**¡SALUD!:** Pair with the Mango-Lime Agua Fresca (page 109).

# CRISPY POTATO TACOS
## *Tacos Dorados de Papa*

Tacos de papa are a Mexican cuisine staple. These crispy taquitos originated in Sinaloa but are famous all over Mexico. These homestyle tacos are tasty, easy to prepare, and inexpensive. Tacos dorados are also popular in Morelos, but there they are called tacos acorazados. These are great paired with Pickled Jalapeños (page 92).

4 medium potatoes, peeled and quartered
4 cups water
Salt
Freshly ground black pepper
12 (6-inch) corn tortillas, warmed
1 cup plus 2 tablespoons shredded Monterey Jack or provolone cheese
1 to 1½ cups corn oil, for frying

GARNISHES
2 cups shredded lettuce
½ cup crumbled queso cotija
½ cup Mexican crema

1. In a medium saucepan, cover the potatoes with the water and boil over medium-high heat. Cover and simmer for 10 to 12 minutes until tender. Drain. Season the potatoes with salt and pepper and mash with a potato masher.

2. Spoon 2 to 3 tablespoons of the mashed potatoes into the middle of each warmed tortilla, and then add cheese to each. Fold each tortilla, forming a taco, or you can roll them to make a taquito.

3. In a large, deep sauté pan or skillet, heat the oil over high heat. Fry the tacos, two or three at a time, for 3 minutes per side, until crisp. Transfer the tacos to a paper-towel-lined plate to drain the excess oil.

4. Serve the tacos hot and garnish with the lettuce, queso cotija, and Mexican crema.

5. Store leftover potato mash in an airtight container in the refrigerator for up to 2 days.

**TIP:** This is a great recipe for leftover mashed potatoes or breakfast potatoes. Use Guajillo Sauce (page 26) for a spicy mashed potato filling.

**¡SALUD!:** Pair with Oatmeal Horchata (page 110).

# CREAMY ZUCCHINI AND CORN TACOS
## *Tacos de Calabacitas con Elote*

Calabacitas is a classic side dish that can also be used for tacos, and it comes together in no time! This recipe is creamy and hearty with spicy notes of roasted green chiles and a pleasant texture thanks to the corn kernels. The cheese is indispensable, as it pairs well with all the ingredients.

1 tablespoon corn oil

½ cup finely chopped white onion

2 medium zucchini, diced

1½ cups frozen corn kernels

1 (4-ounce) can fire-roasted chiles, drained

¼ cup Mexican crema

1 tablespoon chicken bouillon powder

1 teaspoon ground cumin

8 (6-inch) corn or flour tortillas, warmed

### GARNISHES

1 cup shredded Monterey Jack cheese

½ cup Raw Green Salsa (page 94)

1. In a large sauté pan or skillet, heat the oil over medium-high heat until shimmering. Add the onion and sauté for 5 minutes, until it is translucent.

2. Add the zucchini and corn and sauté for about 4 minutes, until the vegetables begin to get tender.

3. Add the chiles, Mexican crema, chicken bouillon, and cumin. Stir and continue cooking for 3 minutes more.

4. Spoon 2 to 3 tablespoons of the zucchini mixture into the middle of each warmed tortilla and fold. Garnish with the cheese and salsa.

5. Store leftover zucchini and corn in an airtight container in the refrigerator for up to 2 days.

¡SALUD!: Pair with the Piña Colada Agua Fresca (page 108).

# CACTUS AND EGG TACOS
## *Tacos de Nopales con Huevo*

A humble ingredient that is now considered a superfood, nopal (cactus) is a part of the indigenous culinary legacy in Mexico. Cactus nopal is a common ingredient found in many Mexican dishes. In Mexico, these breakfast tacos are made with fresh cactus, but it can be challenging to find them in the United States. Luckily, the canned variety is just as delicious.

6 large eggs, at room temperature
1 tablespoon corn oil
¼ cup chopped white onion
2 cups canned nopales, rinsed
Salt
8 (6-inch) corn tortillas or Red Corn Tortillas (page 88)

GARNISH
2 tablespoons Peanut-Arbol Salsa (page 91)

1. Crack the eggs into a medium bowl. Whisk with a fork and set aside.

2. In a medium sauté pan or skillet, heat the oil over medium heat. Sauté the onion for 3 minutes until translucent, then add the nopales. Cook for another 7 to 10 minutes. Season with salt to taste.

3. Pour in the eggs and stir them with a fork. Cook the eggs for no longer than 5 minutes, until set, then remove the skillet from the heat and set it aside.

4. Spoon 2 to 3 tablespoons of the egg mixture into the middle of each warmed tortilla and fold. Garnish with the salsa and serve.

**TIP:** Use canned nopales that are preserved in salted water, not pickled. Some canned nopales come cut into strips, do not chop them. They are very tender, and strips work fine for cooking with the egg scramble.

# MEXICAN EGG SCRAMBLE TACOS
## *Tacos de Huevo à la Mexicana*

Crafting tacos de huevo is a fast and easy way to get a hot breakfast rolled in a tortilla paired with milk and coffee. Egg taquitos have been famous in Texas since the 1900s, thanks to Mexican migrants. You can use the refried beans as a side or add them to your tacos.

6 large eggs, at room temperature

1 tablespoon corn oil

½ cup pico de gallo, freshly made or store-bought

1 teaspoon chicken bouillon powder or salt

1 cup Pinto Beans Two Ways (page 100) or store-bought (optional)

8 (6-inch) flour tortillas, warmed

### GARNISHES

¼ cup shredded Monterey Jack cheese

¼ cup Tomato-Serrano Salsa (page 89)

1. Crack the eggs into a medium bowl. Whisk with a fork and set aside.

2. In a large sauté pan or skillet, heat the oil over medium heat. Sauté the pico de gallo for 3 to 5 minutes and season with the chicken bouillon. Simmer for another minute and add the eggs. Stir to mix in with the salsa, and continue cooking for 5 minutes, until the salsa starts bubbling.

3. Heat the pinto beans on the stovetop or in the microwave.

4. Spoon 1 tablespoon of the warmed refried beans (if using) and 2 tablespoons of cooked eggs into the middle of each warmed tortilla and fold. Garnish each taco with cheese and salsa and serve.

**TIP:** Add 1 tablespoon of sour cream or Greek yogurt for a fluffier egg scramble. Garnish the tacos with Taquero-Style Non-Avocado Guacamole Salsa (page 97) or avocado slices.

**¡SALUD!:** Pair with Mexican Hot Chocolate (page 111).

**TRIVIA:** According to the Austin Eater, Austin is the birthplace of the phrase "breakfast taco."

# GREEN PEA TACOS
## *Tacos Dorados de Chícharo*

These tacos are tasty, and the peas are easy to prepare and available everywhere. Fresh, frozen, or dried peas may be used in these tacos. You can also try them folded in Red Corn Tortillas (page 88).

2 tablespoons salted butter
½ cup chopped white onion
2 garlic cloves, minced
1 (12-ounce) bag frozen peas
1 teaspoon salt
½ teaspoon freshly ground
   black pepper
12 (6-inch) corn tortillas, warmed
½ cup corn oil
2 cups thinly sliced cabbage
1 carrot, shredded
Juice of 1 lime
Salt
Freshly ground black pepper

**GARNISH**
½ cup Tomato-Serrano Salsa
   (page 89)

1. In a large sauté pan, melt the butter over medium heat. Add the onion and cook for 2 minutes, or until translucent. Add the garlic and sauté for 1 minute.

2. Add the peas, stir, and cook for 5 minutes until soft. Season with salt and pepper to taste and cook for 5 to 7 minutes, reducing the liquid. Mash the peas with a potato masher directly in the pan or use a food processor to make a paste.

3. Spoon 2 tablespoons of the mashed pea paste into the middle of each tortilla and fold or roll the tortillas.

4. In a large sauté pan or skillet, heat the oil over high heat. Fry the tacos, two at a time, for 3 minutes on each side until crispy or golden brown. Transfer the tacos to a paper-towel-lined plate to drain the excess oil.

5. In a bowl, mix the cabbage, carrot, and lime juice. Season with salt and pepper to taste and serve the tacos with cabbage slaw and salsa.

6. Store the slaw and pea paste in separate airtight containers in the refrigerator for up to 2 days.

**TIP:** Use dried green or yellow peas instead of frozen. For every 2 cups of dried peas, use 1 cup of water for cooking. That way, the peas will form a paste.

SERVES 6 | **PREP TIME:** 15 minutes | **COOK TIME:** 30 minutes

# HOMEMADE MEXICAN SOY CHORIZO TACOS
## *Tacos de Chorizo de Soya Casero*

The extra-firm tofu in this recipe achieves the same texture as Mexican chorizo. This meatless dish is versatile; enjoy it in tacos and with other Mexican classics such as Mexican Melted Cheese with Chorizo (page 90).

**FOR THE GUAJILLO SAUCE**

4 guajillo peppers, stemmed
  and seeded
1 cup hot water
1 tablespoon corn oil
½ onion, cut into chunks
2 garlic cloves, peeled
1 tablespoon chicken
  bouillon powder
Salt

**FOR THE TACOS**

1 tablespoon corn oil
1 (14-ounce) package extra-firm
  tofu, drained and finely chopped
½ cup chopped white onion
2 garlic cloves, minced
1 teaspoon ground cumin
1 teaspoon dried
  Mexican oregano
1 teaspoon bay leaf powder or
  2 whole leaves
1 teaspoon chicken bouillon
  powder (if needed)
12 (6-inch) corn or flour
  tortillas, warmed
Taquero-Style Non-Avocado
  Guacamole Salsa (page 97)
  (optional)

**TO MAKE THE GUAJILLO SAUCE**

1. In a small bowl, soak the dried peppers in the hot water for 10 to 15 minutes, until soft. Strain, reserving the water.

2. In a medium saucepan, heat the oil over medium heat. Sauté the onion and garlic for about 3 minutes, until browned. Add the guajillos and sauté for 1 minute.

3. Remove from the heat and transfer the mixture to a blender. Add the chicken bouillon and ½ cup of the pepper-soaking water. Blend until smooth.

4. Pour the sauce back into the saucepan, and cook for 7 minutes, adding more water if needed, until the consistency of the sauce is thick. Season with salt.

**TO MAKE THE TACOS**

5. In a Dutch oven or a Mexican clay pot, heat the oil over medium heat. Sauté the tofu for 2 to 3 minutes, add the onion and garlic, and stir. Continue cooking for 3 minutes, until the onion is softened.

6. Add the cumin, oregano, and bay leaf powder. Cook for 1 to 2 minutes and continue stirring.

7. Pour in the guajillo sauce and season with more chicken bouillon if needed. Reduce the heat to low, cover, and cook the soy chorizo for 3 more minutes.

8. Remove the lid, taste, and allow the soy chorizo to reduce the liquid. It could take another 5 to 10 minutes, depending on the thickness of the guajillo sauce.

9. Spoon 2 to 3 tablespoons of soy chorizo into the middle of each warmed tortilla and fold. Garnish with the guacamole salsa (if using).

10. Store leftover soy chorizo in an airtight container in the refrigerator for up to 3 days.

● ● ● ● ● ● ● ● ● ● ● ● ● ● ● ● ● ● ● ● ● ● ● ● ● ● ● ● ● ● ● ● ● ● ● ● ● ● ● ● ● ● ● ● ● ●

**¡SALUD!:** Pair with Mango Mezcal Mojitos (page 106).

● ● ● ● ● ● ● ● ● ● ● ● ● ● ● ● ● ● ● ● ● ● ● ● ● ● ● ● ● ● ● ● ● ● ● ● ● ● ● ● ● ● ● ● ● ●

# QUESO FRESCO CRISPY TACOS
## *Tacos Dorados de Queso Fresco*

The queso fresco crispy tacos are known as *sopa de tacos,* or tacos soup, because a serving of crispy tacos comes with a bowl of spicy tomato broth used to dip the tacos and spoon some broth in between. This way of eating tacos is comforting and a lunchtime staple. I grew up eating tacos this way at home. You'll love them!

12 slices queso fresco, firm, not crumbly
12 (6-inch) corn tortillas, warmed
1 cup corn oil
4 cups warm (or hot) Spicy Tomato Broth for Tacos (page 93)

1. Place 1 slice of queso fresco in the middle of each tortilla. Roll each tortilla, using a wooden skewer or toothpick to secure them, and set aside.

2. In a large, deep sauté pan or skillet, heat the oil over high heat. Fry the tacos, two at a time, for 2 minutes per side, until crisp. Transfer the tacos to a paper-towel-lined plate to drain the excess oil.

3. Serve the tacos hot alongside a bowl of the spicy broth for dipping.

**TIP:** Slightly fry the tortillas instead of warming them in the comal. That will make it easier to roll them tightly if you don't want to use wooden toothpicks. First fry the tortilla on one side and press it with a turner spatula until crispy, then turn again to fry the other side until golden brown.

# CRISPY CARROT TACOS
## *Tacos Dorados de Zanahoria*

The crispy carrot tacos are a staple for meatless Friday and Lent in Mexico. The chipotle sauce provides a nice smoky note that makes the sweetness of the carrot shine. This kind of taco is simple to prepare and inexpensive.

1 tablespoon salted butter

¼ cup finely chopped white onion

1 garlic clove, minced

1 teaspoon ground cumin

4 large carrots, shredded

¼ cup vegetable broth

1 teaspoon chipotle sauce

½ teaspoon salt

12 (6-inch) corn tortillas, warmed

½ cup corn oil

**GARNISHES**

2 cups shredded romaine lettuce

½ cup Mexican crema

½ cup crumbled cotija cheese

4 radishes, thinly sliced

½ cup Drunken Salsa (page 99)

1. In a sauté pan, heat the butter on medium heat. Add the onion and sauté for 2 minutes, until translucent.

2. Add the garlic and cumin and stir for about 1 minute, until fragrant. Then add the carrots, vegetable broth, and chipotle sauce and stir to combine. Cover and cook for 10 to 12 minutes, until the carrots become tender. Add salt to taste.

3. Spoon 2 to 3 tablespoons of the carrot mixture into the middle of each tortilla. Fold and set aside.

4. In a large sauté pan or skillet, heat the oil over high heat. Fry the tacos, two at a time, for 3 minutes per side, until crisp. Transfer the tacos to a paper-towel-lined plate to drain the excess oil.

5. Serve the tacos garnished with the lettuce, Mexican crema, cotija cheese, radishes, and salsa. Store leftover carrot mixture in an airtight container in the refrigerator for up to 2 days.

**TIP:** Use pre-shredded carrots to reduce prep time. Replace the butter with vegan butter or olive oil, the Mexican crema with vegan sour cream, and the cotija cheese with vegan Parmesan cheese for a vegan version. Replace the chipotle sauce with paprika.

# VEGAN LENTIL TACOS
## *Tacos Veganos de Lentejas*

Many taco lovers who embrace a vegan diet are looking for tasty meals that remind them of home. Thus, vegan tacos are very popular. Using the same flavor profile as Mexican picadillo, I have veganized this classic. Lentils are a suitable replacement for ground beef and make a delightful vegan picadillo.

**FOR THE LENTILS**

2 cups brown lentils, rinsed

1 teaspoon salt

2 to 3 cups water

**FOR THE PICADILLO**

1 tablespoon coconut oil

½ cup chopped white onion

3 garlic cloves, minced

2 Roma tomatoes, diced

2 cups frozen peas and carrot mix

¼ cup vegetable broth

2 tablespoons chipotle sauce

2 tablespoons taco seasoning

½ teaspoon salt

12 (6-inch) corn tortillas, warmed

**GARNISHES**

2 cups shredded romaine lettuce

2 large avocados, mashed

1 cup Street Taco Salsa (page 98)

**TO MAKE THE LENTILS**

1. In a medium saucepan, combine the lentils and salt over medium heat, and cover with the water. Bring to a boil, then lower the heat to low and cover.

2. Cook for 10 minutes until al dente, not mushy. Check on them every 5 minutes to ensure you have not overcooked them. Drain any excess liquid, rinse with cold water, and set aside.

**TO MAKE THE PICADILLO**

3. In a Dutch oven, heat the oil over medium heat and sauté the onion for 2 minutes until translucent. Add the garlic and sauté for 1 minute until fragrant. Add the diced tomatoes, 2 cups of cooked lentils, and the peas and carrot mix.

4. Pour in the vegetable broth, chipotle sauce, taco seasoning, and salt. Stir and cover with the lid. Lower the heat to low and cook for 10 minutes to allow the flavors to develop. Check from time to time and add more vegetable broth if needed. Be mindful that the dish is not watery and that lentils must keep their shape and not be mushy.

5. Spoon 2 to 3 tablespoons of the lentil picadillo into the middle of each tortilla and fold. Garnish with the lettuce, avocado mash, and salsa.

6. Store leftover picadillo in an airtight container in the refrigerator for up to 4 days.

• • • • • • • • • • • • • • • • • • • • • • • • • • • • • • • • • • • • • • • • • • • • • • • • • • •

**TIP:** Use green lentils or French puy lentils, and cook them the day before, as those take 45 minutes to cook but are firmer and do not lose their shape quickly. This recipe is freezer-friendly, too.

• • • • • • • • • • • • • • • • • • • • • • • • • • • • • • • • • • • • • • • • • • • • • • • • • • •

**TRIVIA:** Mexican cuisine embraces meatless options. Aztecs used to stuff corn tortillas with chile peppers, squash, cactus, and mushrooms even before the conquest.

• • • • • • • • • • • • • • • • • • • • • • • • • • • • • • • • • • • • • • • • • • • • • • • • • • •

# VEGAN "EGG" SCRAMBLE TACOS
## *Tacos Veganos de Huevo*

Those who follow a vegan diet will be happy to know that you can still eat plenty of tacos. The "eggs" in this recipe come together using tofu and nutritional yeast. That is the secret to an eggy, cheesy flavor. These vegan tacos go well with gluten-free tortillas of your choice, and easily pair with your favorite salsas and garnishes. The combinations are endless!

1 (14- or 16-ounce) firm tofu block, drained

1 tablespoon coconut oil

2 tablespoons nutritional yeast

1 teaspoon garlic powder

½ teaspoon ground turmeric

2 tablespoons nondairy milk

1 teaspoon salt

Pinch freshly ground black pepper

12 (6-inch) flour or corn tortillas, warmed

**GARNISHES**

1 cup pico de gallo

2 small avocados, mashed

1. Finely break down the raw tofu in a food processor or using a potato masher. Strain and press it using a fine colander or cheesecloth to remove excess liquid.

2. In a large sauté pan, heat the oil over medium heat. Add the tofu and stir for 3 to 4 minutes, until the rest of the water from the tofu evaporates.

3. Add the nutritional yeast, garlic powder, and turmeric, and stir again. Cook for another 5 to 7 minutes. Incorporate the milk and stir again. Season with salt and pepper to taste. Set aside.

4. Spoon 2 tablespoons of the tofu scramble into the middle of each warmed tortilla and fold. Garnish with the pico de gallo and avocado mash and serve.

**TIP:** Tofu comes in 14- or 16-ounce blocks; both work for this recipe. Replace the turmeric with curry powder for a spicy note. Replace nutritional yeast with coconut aminos or soy sauce.

## CHAPTER 3

# CHICKEN

‹ Chicken Flautas or Taquitos, page 43

# COLA CHICKEN THIGHS TACOS
## *Tacos de Pollo à la Coca Cola*

This recipe for cola chicken has the perfect balance of sweet, spicy, and smoky. And chicken thighs are the ideal meat to use as they are flavorful, juicy, tender, and easy to shred. Hickory or brown-sugar barbecue sauce works best in this recipe.

6 boneless, skinless chicken thighs (1 pound)

½ teaspoon salt

½ teaspoon freshly ground black pepper

1 teaspoon corn oil

1 (12-ounce) can cola

1 (6-ounce) can tomato paste

½ onion, coarsely chopped

3 tablespoons barbecue sauce

2 canned chipotles adobados, plus 2 teaspoons of the sauce

1 tablespoon seasoning sauce (Jugo Maggi) or soy sauce

1 tablespoon chicken bouillon powder

2 garlic cloves, peeled

¼ cup water or chicken broth

12 (6-inch) corn or flour tortillas, warmed

**GARNISHES**

1 cup finely shredded cabbage

½ cup shredded carrots

½ cup coarsely chopped fresh cilantro

Juice of 1 lime

1 teaspoon salt

1. Pat the chicken thighs dry with paper towels and season them with salt and pepper on both sides.

2. Pour the oil into an Instant Pot and select the Sauté mode. Heat the oil for 1 to 2 minutes until shimmering.

3. Sear the seasoned chicken thighs for 2 to 3 minutes on both sides, until lightly browned. Turn off the Sauté mode.

4. Add the cola, tomato paste, onion, barbecue sauce, chipotle and sauce, seasoning sauce, chicken bouillon, and garlic to a blender. Blend for 1 to 2 minutes until the sauce reaches a smooth consistency.

5. Pour the sauce on the chicken, add the water, and mix.

6. Close the lid and cook the chicken on high pressure for 15 minutes. When done cooking, allow the pressure to release naturally.

7. Carefully remove the lid, shred the chicken using two forks, and mix it into the sauce.

8. Spoon 2 to 3 tablespoons of the filling into the middle of each tortilla and fold. Garnish the tacos with cabbage, carrots, cilantro, lime, and salt. Include a side of Mexican Red Rice (page 95) for a complete meal.

9. Store leftover chicken in an airtight container in the refrigerator for up to 3 days.

∙ ∙ ∙ ∙ ∙ ∙ ∙ ∙ ∙ ∙ ∙ ∙ ∙ ∙ ∙ ∙ ∙ ∙ ∙ ∙ ∙ ∙ ∙ ∙ ∙ ∙ ∙ ∙ ∙ ∙ ∙ ∙ ∙ ∙ ∙ ∙ ∙ ∙ ∙ ∙ ∙ ∙ ∙ ∙ ∙ ∙ ∙ ∙ ∙ ∙

**¡SALUD!:** Pair with the Mango-Lime Agua Fresca (page 109).

∙ ∙ ∙ ∙ ∙ ∙ ∙ ∙ ∙ ∙ ∙ ∙ ∙ ∙ ∙ ∙ ∙ ∙ ∙ ∙ ∙ ∙ ∙ ∙ ∙ ∙ ∙ ∙ ∙ ∙ ∙ ∙ ∙ ∙ ∙ ∙ ∙ ∙ ∙ ∙ ∙ ∙ ∙ ∙ ∙ ∙ ∙ ∙ ∙ ∙

**TRIVIA:** One of the first exposures to tacos for Americans was through Mexican food carts in Los Angeles ran by the Chili Queens, a women-run business.

∙ ∙ ∙ ∙ ∙ ∙ ∙ ∙ ∙ ∙ ∙ ∙ ∙ ∙ ∙ ∙ ∙ ∙ ∙ ∙ ∙ ∙ ∙ ∙ ∙ ∙ ∙ ∙ ∙ ∙ ∙ ∙ ∙ ∙ ∙ ∙ ∙ ∙ ∙ ∙ ∙ ∙ ∙ ∙ ∙ ∙ ∙ ∙ ∙ ∙

# SPICY PRUNE SAUCE SHREDDED CHICKEN TACOS

## *Tacos de Pollo en Salsa de Ciruela y Pasilla*

Spanish nuns that came to Puebla during the viceroyship brought recipes from the Old World and adapted them using local ingredients to create dishes like the now-classic pork in prune sauce, a dish used as the inspiration for this recipe.

**FOR THE PRUNE SAUCE**

6 prunes, pitted

2 pasilla peppers, stemmed and seeded

1 cup hot water

2 tablespoons packed light brown sugar

2 tablespoons seasoning sauce (Jugo Maggi) or soy sauce

1 tablespoon chicken bouillon powder

2 garlic cloves, peeled

**FOR THE CHICKEN TACOS**

6 boneless, skinless chicken thighs (1 pound)

1 tablespoon ground cumin

½ teaspoon salt

½ teaspoon freshly ground black pepper

1 teaspoon corn oil

¼ cup chicken broth or water

12 (6-inch) corn or flour tortillas, warmed

**GARNISHES**

½ cup Peanut-Arbol Salsa (page 91) or Habanero Red Onion Salsa (page 102)

½ cup chopped fresh cilantro

**TO MAKE THE PRUNE SAUCE**

1. In a small saucepan, soak the prunes and the pasilla peppers in the hot water for 10 minutes, until soft. Strain, reserving the water.

2. Add the soaked peppers, prunes, 1 cup of the pepper-soaking water, brown sugar, seasoning sauce, chicken bouillon, and garlic to a blender. Blend for 2 minutes until the sauce becomes smooth. Set aside.

**TO MAKE THE CHICKEN TACOS**

3. Pat the chicken thighs dry with paper towels and season with cumin, salt, and pepper on both sides.

4. Pour the oil into an Instant Pot and select the Sauté mode. Heat the oil for 1 to 2 minutes until shimmering.

5. Transfer the chicken to the Instant Pot, and sear for 2 to 3 minutes on each side, until lightly browned. Turn off the Sauté mode.

6. Pour the prune sauce over the chicken thighs, add the broth, and mix.

7. Close the lid and cook the chicken on high pressure for 15 minutes. When done cooking, allow the pressure to release naturally.

8.  Carefully remove the lid, shred the chicken using two forks, and mix it into the sauce.

9.  Spoon 2 to 3 tablespoons of the filling into the middle of each tortilla and fold. Garnish the tacos with the salsa and cilantro. Store leftover chicken in an airtight container in the refrigerator for up to 3 days.

· · · · · · · · · · · · · · · · · · · · · · · · · · · · · · · · · · · · · · · · · · · · · ·

**¡SALUD!:** Pair with Oatmeal Horchata (page 110).

· · · · · · · · · · · · · · · · · · · · · · · · · · · · · · · · · · · · · · · · · · · · · ·

**TRIVIA:** In 1920, tacos became a Mexican-American fusion. Cheddar cheese, cool lettuce, and tomato became standard fare for tacos.

· · · · · · · · · · · · · · · · · · · · · · · · · · · · · · · · · · · · · · · · · · · · · ·

# CHICKEN TINGA TACOS
## *Tacos de Tinga de Pollo*

The word *tinga* means stew. This dish is part of the legacy left by the Spanish nuns, and it's a staple of Poblano cuisine. Chicken tinga is one of those dishes commonly served in tacos de guisado. These tacos became famous in Morelos, Puebla, and Mexico City. Nowadays, everyone eats them nationwide because any guisado can go inside a taco.

½ cup Spanish-style chorizo, removed from casing and sliced

½ medium white onion, sliced

1 garlic clove, chopped

2 cups shredded rotisserie chicken

1 roasted red pepper, chopped

1 cup tomato puree

½ cup water or chicken stock

2 canned chipotle peppers, chopped

1 tablespoon chicken bouillon powder

1 teaspoon salt

½ teaspoon freshly ground black pepper

12 (6-inch) corn or flour tortillas, warmed

### GARNISHES

1 avocado, sliced

1 cup Pickled Jalapeños (page 92)

1. In a Dutch oven, cook the chorizo over medium heat for 5 minutes, until browned. Drain the excess fat, then return to the heat. Add the onion and garlic and sauté for 2 minutes until the onion is translucent.

2. Add the shredded chicken, red pepper, and tomato puree, stirring to combine.

3. Mix in the water, chipotle peppers, and chicken bouillon. Cover and cook for another 3 minutes, until bubbling. Taste and add salt and pepper if needed.

4. Spoon 2 to 3 tablespoons of chicken tinga into each tortilla and fold. Top with the avocado slices and serve with the Pickled Jalapeños. Store leftover chicken in an airtight container in the refrigerator for up to 3 days.

**TIP:** Classic tinga does include chorizo. It could be replaced with bacon or omitted altogether. Use a rotisserie chicken from the store to ease the prep time. This guisado is freezer-friendly. Leftovers keep fresh for up to 4 days in an airtight container inside the refrigerator.

**¡SALUD!:** Pair with the Piña Colada Agua Fresca (page 108).

# SHREDDED PANFRIED CHICKEN TACOS WITH ONIONS
## *Tacos de Pollo Frito con Cebolla*

Tacos are excellent for repurposing leftovers. I took inspiration from the famous tacos de machaca and chicken leftovers. But instead of using beef, I am using rotisserie chicken. The trick to these tacos is that the chicken is fried with onions until golden brown. The flavor is fantastic and makes an excellent option for a quick dinner.

2 tablespoons corn oil
1 cup shredded rotisserie chicken
½ cup thinly sliced white onion
1 tablespoon salt
½ teaspoon freshly ground
    black pepper
1 jalapeño, seeded and julienned
8 (6-inch) corn or flour
    tortillas, warmed

**GARNISHES**
1 lime, quartered
1 cup Taquero-Style
    Non-Avocado Guacamole
    Salsa (page 97)

1. In a large sauté pan or skillet, heat the oil over high heat for 1 to 2 minutes. Lower the heat to medium and add the chicken, onion, salt, and pepper, and fry for 10 minutes, stirring occasionally.

2. Add the jalapeño and fry for another 2 minutes. The chicken will be ready when it is crispy and the onion turns golden brown.

3. Spoon 2 to 3 tablespoons of fried chicken mix into the middle of each tortilla and fold. Garnish with a few drops of lime juice and the salsa. Store leftover chicken in an airtight container in the refrigerator for up to 2 days.

**TIP:** Any shredded meat is suitable with this recipe. Just make sure the meat is dry and not wet. Or make it vegetarian by replacing the chicken with mushrooms.

# CHICKEN SKEWER TACOS
## *Tacos de Alambre de Pollo*

The word *alambre* means skewers. These tacos are a taquería staple, and some come with chicken, beef, or pork and are topped with melted cheese. These are grilled over a direct flame using a charcoal grill, but they can also be cooked on the stovetop in a cast-iron sauté pan, and no skewers are necessary.

2 (8-ounce) boneless, skinless chicken breasts, cut into 3-inch chunks

1 tablespoon chicken bouillon powder

1 teaspoon freshly ground black pepper

1 tablespoon corn oil or pork lard

½ medium red onion, sliced

1 green bell pepper, seeded and thinly sliced

1 red bell pepper, seeded and thinly sliced

1 cup cooked, crumbled Mexican chorizo (optional)

1½ cups shredded Monterey Jack cheese

12 (6-inch) corn or flour tortillas, warmed

### GARNISH

½ cup Tomato-Serrano Salsa (page 89) or Raw Green Salsa (page 94)

1. Pat the chicken dry with paper towels. Place in a medium bowl, season with the chicken bouillon and the pepper, and set aside.

2. In a large cast-iron sauté pan, heat the oil over high heat. When the oil is hot, add the chicken and cook for 8 to 10 minutes, until browned. Lower the heat to medium and add the red onion and green and red pepper. Cook for 5 to 7 minutes, until softened, then add the cooked chorizo (if using). Stir and cook for another 2 minutes.

3. Top with the cheese, turn the heat off, and cover the pan with a lid for 2 minutes to allow the cheese to melt and become queso fundido.

4. Spoon 2 tablespoons of the chicken alambre into the middle of each tortilla and fold. Garnish with the salsa. Store leftover chicken in an airtight container in the refrigerator for up to 2 days.

**TIP:** Any lean meat is suitable for alambres. Try them with steak or pork loin. Replace the chorizo with bacon. Bring the pan to the table and enjoy family style.

**¡SALUD!:** Pair with an ice-cold beer or a Classic Lime Margarita (page 117).

# CHICKEN FLAUTAS OR TAQUITOS
## *Flautas de Pollo*

Flautas de pollo are crispy, tightly rolled tacos served with fresh, thinly sliced romaine lettuce, Mexican crema, crumbled cotija cheese, and guacamole salsa. The texture is crunchy and delicious and is an authentic street taco initiated in Mexico City. Use store-bought rotisserie chicken to make this a quick meal.

12 large (6-inch) corn tortillas
3 cups shredded
   rotisserie chicken
1 cup corn oil

**GARNISHES**
3 cups shredded romaine lettuce
1 cup Taquero-Style
   Non-Avocado Guacamole
   Salsa (page 97)
½ cup crumbled queso cotija
1 cup Mexican crema

1. In a comal or large nonstick skillet, heat the tortillas over medium heat for 30 to 45 seconds on each side, until soft and pliable, and transfer them to a platter. If the tortillas are too stiff, do a quick fry to soften and transfer them to a plate to stuff them with the shredded chicken.

2. Add 2 tablespoons of chicken to the center of each tortilla and roll tightly. Repeat this step with all the tortillas and set them aside.

3. In a large, deep sauté pan or skillet, heat the oil over high heat. Fry the flautas, three at a time, for about 3 minutes per side, until crispy. Transfer the finished flautas to a paper-towel-covered plate to absorb the excess oil.

4. Serve warm, garnished with the lettuce, guacamole salsa, queso cotija, and Mexican crema. Store leftover chicken in an airtight container in the refrigerator for up to 2 days.

**TIP:** You can stuff flautas with other ingredients or leftovers, such as potato, cheese, shredded beef, or carnitas. Prepare the flautas a day in advance but wait to fry them until they're ready to eat as they tend to get soggy. Non-fried flautas are freezer-friendly. Just vacuum seal to attain freshness.

**¡SALUD!:** Pair with a Chamoy Michelada (page 112).

# CHICKEN LIME TACOS
## *Tacos de Pollo al Limón*

In Mexican cuisine, lime is a must. We use it for almost everything: marinades, drinks, and desserts. We even add a lime wedge when serving tacos. The secret for the best flavor resides in the lime marinade and the grilling technique.

½ cup freshly squeezed
  lime juice
1 tablespoon seasoning sauce
  (Jugo Maggi) or soy sauce
2 (8-ounce) boneless, skinless
  chicken breasts
1 tablespoon ground cumin
1 teaspoon chicken
  bouillon powder
1 teaspoon freshly ground
  black pepper
1 tablespoon corn oil
8 (6-inch) corn tortillas, warmed

**GARNISHES**
1 cup finely chopped red onion
½ cup coarsely chopped fresh
  cilantro
3 limes, cut into wedges
1 cup Raw Green Salsa (page 94)

1. In a mixing bowl, combine the lime juice and the seasoning sauce. Submerge the chicken in the marinade and cover with plastic wrap. Marinate for a minimum of 30 minutes in the refrigerator.

2. Remove the chicken from the marinade, pat it dry with a paper towel, and season with the cumin, chicken bouillon, and pepper.

3. Heat a cast-iron grill pan over high heat. Once hot, lower the heat to medium and coat with the oil. Grill the chicken for 8 to 10 minutes on each side, until cooked through. Remove it using tongs and let it rest for 2 to 3 minutes.

4. Chop the grilled chicken, place 2 to 3 tablespoons into the middle of each tortilla, and fold. Garnish with the red onion, cilantro, lime, and salsa. Store leftover chicken in an airtight container in the refrigerator for up to 2 days.

**TRIVIA:** As of the printing of this book, the largest taco recorded by Guinness World Records was made in Mexicali, Baja California, Mexico, and weighed 1,654 pounds!

# CHICKEN MOLE TACOS
## *Tacos de Pollo con Mole*

Mole is a crown jewel of Mexican cuisine. It best represents how two cultures, the Spanish and the Mexican, come together in a magical sauce likely created in the seventeenth century by Sister Andrea de la Asunción from the convent of Santa Rosa in Puebla. Chicken mole is another staple for what is known as tacos de guisado, typical for parties. Good-quality mole paste and Mexican chocolate can be found at Amazon, Whole Foods, or Walmart.

1 cup mole paste
1 to 2 cups chicken broth
1 (3-ounce) Mexican chocolate tablet, cut into pieces
4 cups shredded rotisserie chicken
12 (6-inch) corn or flour tortillas, warmed

**GARNISH**
¼ cup toasted sesame seeds

1. In a large saucepan over medium heat, add the mole paste and 1 cup of chicken broth. Stir and cook the mole until dissolved, about 7 minutes.

2. Add the Mexican chocolate and more chicken broth if necessary. Keep stirring to prevent the mixture from sticking to the bottom of the saucepan. The sauce will become thicker with a gravy-like consistency.

3. Add the shredded chicken, mix with the mole sauce, and cook for another 3 to 4 minutes. Cover with a lid and remove from the heat.

4. Spoon 2 to 3 tablespoons of the chicken mole into the middle of each tortilla and fold. Garnish with the toasted sesame seeds and serve with a side of warm Mexican Red Rice (page 95). Store leftover chicken in an airtight container in the refrigerator for up to 3 days.

**TIP:** Use rotisserie chicken or drained canned chicken. Choose Poblano (red) or Oaxacan-style (black) mole. For an authentic cooking experience, use a Mexican clay pot.

**¡SALUD!:** Pair with the Mango-Lime Agua Fresca (page 109).

# CHICKEN PASTOR TACOS
## *Tacos de Pollo al Pastor*

Tacos al Pastor are one of the top-ten most-sought tacos in Mexico City. Classic pastor is made with pork steaks and cooked on a trompo-style grill. This chicken version uses these beloved classic tacos as the inspiration. The preparation uses the same condiments, the process is simple, and the taco is still full of flavor.

½ cup freshly squeezed orange juice

½ (3½-ounce) package achiote paste

2 tablespoons apple cider vinegar

1 teaspoon dried Mexican oregano

1 teaspoon ground cumin

6 thin chicken steaks (1 pound) (see Tip, page 47)

1 tablespoon corn oil

12 (6-inch) corn tortillas, warmed

### GARNISHES

6 pineapple slices

½ cup Habanero Red Onion Salsa (page 102)

½ cup chopped fresh cilantro

3 limes, quartered

1. Put the orange juice, achiote paste, apple cider vinegar, oregano, and cumin in a blender and process until smooth. (You can also dilute the paste in a small bowl and mix using a fork.)

2. Place the chicken steaks in a large bowl and coat them with the achiote marinade. Cover the bowl with plastic wrap and marinate in the refrigerator for 30 minutes or overnight. The more you marinate, the better the flavor will develop.

3. Place a large cast-iron grill pan over high heat. Once hot, lower the heat to medium and coat the pan with the oil.

4. Grill the chicken steaks and cook on each side for 3 to 5 minutes, or until grill marks appear and the internal temperature reaches 170°F.

5. Let the chicken steaks rest for 2 to 3 minutes before slicing and chopping.

6.  Sear the pineapple slices for 1 to 2 minutes on each side over high heat using the same grilling skillet used for the chicken. Cut the grilled slices into chunks.

7.  Spoon 2 tablespoons of chopped al pastor chicken into the middle of each tortilla and fold. Garnish with the pineapple, salsa, cilantro, and limes. Store leftover chicken in an airtight container in the refrigerator for up to 2 days.

• • • • • • • • • • • • • • • • • • • • • • • • • • • • • • • • • • • • • • • • • • •

**TIP:** For the best flavor, use deboned, skinned chicken thighs. This chicken cut is juicy and best suited for cooking and overnight marinating. Flatten the chicken thighs using two plastic sheets and a tenderizer.

• • • • • • • • • • • • • • • • • • • • • • • • • • • • • • • • • • • • • • • • • • •

**¡SALUD!:** Pair with Classic Lime Margaritas (page 117).

• • • • • • • • • • • • • • • • • • • • • • • • • • • • • • • • • • • • • • • • • • •

# GRILLED ADOBO CHICKEN TACOS
## *Tacos de Pollo Asado en Adobo*

In Mexico, adobo means a thick sauce of dried peppers, spices, and vinegar essential for an authentic Mexican adobo. Typically, adobo uses guajillo, ancho, and pasilla peppers and pairs primarily with pork and chicken but can be used for seafood and fish. The adobo flavor is mild and smoky, not too spicy. The pollo asado estilo Sinaloa is the inspiration for the grilled adobo chicken tacos with the spicy kick of the chile de árbol.

4 (4-ounce) boneless, skinless chicken thighs, flattened

1 teaspoon salt

2 guajillo peppers, stemmed and seeded

1 chile de árbol, stemmed and seeded (optional)

2 cups hot water

¼ cup apple cider vinegar

1 tablespoon ground cumin

1 tablespoon chicken bouillon powder

1 teaspoon dried Mexican oregano

1 teaspoon garlic powder

1 teaspoon freshly ground black pepper

1 tablespoon corn oil

12 (6-inch) corn tortillas, warmed

### GARNISHES

½ cup Peanut-Arbol Salsa (page 91)

½ cup chopped fresh cilantro

3 limes, quartered

1. Pat the chicken thighs dry with paper towels and season them with salt. Set them aside, cover, and refrigerate until ready to cook.

2. In a small sauté pan or skillet, roast the guajillo and chile de árbol (if using) over medium heat for 10 to 12 seconds to avoid burning them. The roasting is necessary for waking up the flavor of the pepper.

3. Add the hot water to the skillet and soak the chiles for 10 minutes, until soft. Strain, reserving the water.

4. Put the softened peppers, 3 tablespoons of the pepper-soaking water, the apple cider vinegar, the cumin, the chicken bouillon, the oregano, the garlic powder, and the pepper in a blender. Blend for 2 to 3 minutes until achieving a smooth, not-watery sauce.

5. Pour the adobo into a mixing bowl and marinate the chicken thighs in the sauce for 15 minutes before cooking.

6. Place a large cast-iron grill pan over high heat and coat with the oil. Lower the heat to medium high.

7. Cook the chicken on each side for 8 to 10 minutes, or until grill marks appear, and the internal temperature reaches 170°F.

8. Allow the chicken to rest for 2 to 3 minutes before chopping.

9. Spoon 2 to 3 tablespoons of adobo chicken into the middle of each tortilla and fold. Garnish the tacos with the salsa, cilantro, and lime juice. Store leftover chicken in an airtight container in the refrigerator for up to 3 days.

• • • • • • • • • • • • • • • • • • • • • • • • • • • • • • • • • • • • • • • • • • •

**TIP:** Flatten the chicken thighs using two plastic sheets and a tenderizer. Or ask the staff at the meat counter to process the chicken for you.

• • • • • • • • • • • • • • • • • • • • • • • • • • • • • • • • • • • • • • • • • • •

**TRIVIA:** *Taquería* is the Spanish word for a taco shop. We know the taquera culture started in Mexico City, but there is no certainty about when tacos were invented.

• • • • • • • • • • • • • • • • • • • • • • • • • • • • • • • • • • • • • • • • • • •

# CHAPTER 4

## SEAFOOD

 Governor Shrimp Tacos, page 53

# SHRIMP MACHACA TACOS
## *Tacos de Machaca de Camarón*

Seafood machaca is a traditional dish from Sinaloa made with either cooked shrimp or fish. The dish's name, machaca, or crushes, comes from crushing the cooked shrimp using a mortar instead of cutting. These tacos go great with a side of Pinto Beans Two Ways (page 100).

1 tablespoon corn oil

1 cup finely chopped onion

2 Anaheim peppers, seeded and finely chopped

1 serrano pepper, finely chopped (optional)

2 garlic cloves, peeled

1 cup diced Roma tomatoes

2 bay leaves

1 teaspoon dried Mexican oregano

1 teaspoon or 1 cube shrimp bouillon powder

½ teaspoon dried thyme

½ cup water

1 pound medium shrimp, peeled, deveined, and cooked

¼ teaspoon freshly ground black pepper

Salt (optional)

Juice of 1 Persian lime

12 (6-inch) flour tortillas, warmed

**GARNISHES**

½ cup Peanut-Arbol Salsa (page 91)

2 limes, quartered

1. In a medium sauté pan or skillet, heat the corn oil over medium-high heat and sauté the onion for 1 to 2 minutes, or until the onion turns translucent. Add the Anaheim peppers, serrano pepper (if using), and garlic and cook for 1 minute.

2. Add the tomatoes, bay leaves, oregano, shrimp bouillon, and thyme. Add the water and stir. Cover the skillet and allow the sauce to cook over medium-low heat for 10 minutes until the tomatoes are soft. Remove from the heat and keep it covered.

3. On a chopping block, use a meat tenderizer to crush the shrimp one at a time. The shrimp will come apart, resulting in shredded shrimp meat. In a bowl, mix the shrimp with the sauce, pepper, and salt (if using). Squeeze the Persian lime over the mixture and mix well.

4. Spoon 2 tablespoons of machaca into the middle of each tortilla and fold. Garnish with the salsa and lime quarters and serve.

**TIP:** Use precooked frozen shrimp and defrost inside the refrigerator the night before. Use the food processor to cut the shrimp.

# GOVERNOR SHRIMP TACOS
## *Tacos Gobernador de Camarón*

There are many stories about how the Tacos Gobernador came about, but everyone knows these shrimp tacos are a delight and a Sinaloa staple. The combination with the buttery shrimp, roasted poblano peppers, and the cheese is full of flavor and the perfect filling for a one-of-a-kind taco worthy of a governor's palate.

2 tablespoons unsalted butter

1 tablespoon corn oil

1 cup thinly sliced white onion

2 poblano peppers, stemmed, seeded, roasted, peeled, and chopped

3 Roma tomatoes, diced

1 tablespoon chicken bouillon powder

2 garlic cloves, minced

½ teaspoon freshly ground black pepper

1 pound large shrimp, peeled and deveined

2 cups shredded Monterey Jack cheese

12 (6-inch) flour or corn tortillas, warmed

### GARNISHES

½ cup Tomato–Serrano Salsa (page 89)

1 large avocado, sliced

1. In a large sauté pan or skillet, heat the butter and the oil over medium-high heat, and sauté the onion and the poblano peppers for 2 minutes. Add the tomatoes, chicken bouillon, garlic, and pepper.

2. Lower to medium heat, and allow the sofrito to simmer for 2 minutes, or until the tomatoes become soft and the sauce starts bubbling.

3. Add the shrimp and cook for a maximum of 2 minutes with constant stirring.

4. Turn off the heat and add the cheese. Cover and let the cheese melt for 1 to 2 minutes.

5. Spoon 2 to 3 tablespoons of the cheesy shrimp into the middle of each tortilla and fold. Garnish with the salsa and avocado slices and serve.

**TIP:** Use peeled and deveined frozen shrimp and defrost inside the refrigerator the night before. When the shrimp turns pink while cooking, it's ready, and it's overcooked if it curls.

# BROILED LOBSTER TACOS
## *Tacos de Langosta à la Parrilla*

The lobster tacos recipe is a classic from Puerto Nuevo's Rosarito Beach in Baja, California. The lobster is abundant in this area known as "the lobster village." The grilled lobster taco recipe originated in 1956 and was created by a fisherman's wife who first cooked it for tourists visiting the site.

4 lobster tails

¼ cup unsalted butter, at room temperature

1 teaspoon ground cumin

1 teaspoon garlic powder

1 teaspoon salt

1 teaspoon freshly ground black pepper

12 (6-inch) corn tortillas, warmed

**GARNISHES**

1 cup Tomato-Serrano Salsa (page 89)

1 cup chopped fresh cilantro

2 limes, quartered

1. Preheat the oven to broil at 500°F.

2. Cut the top of each lobster tail with seafood scissors, pull the meat up, and set the shell aside.

3. Spread 1 tablespoon of butter on each lobster tail, making sure to cover all the meat with the butter.

4. In a small bowl, mix the cumin, garlic powder, salt, and pepper and sprinkle this spice mix over each lobster tail.

5. Place the lobster meat back in the shells and put the shells on a baking sheet and broil for 5 to 10 minutes. Do not exceed this cooking time to avoid overcooking. The lobsters are ready when they turn pink and are reaching an internal temperature between 140°F and 145°F.

6. Remove the lobsters from the oven and let cool for 2 minutes. Remove the cooked meat from the shell and cut it into chunks.

7. Place a few chunks of the broiled lobster into the middle of each tortilla and fold. Garnish with the salsa and cilantro, add a few drops of lime juice, and serve.

**TIP:** Ask the fishmonger to cut and prep the lobster tails for broiling, which saves you time and the need to use seafood scissors. Frozen lobsters are acceptable if fresh ones are not readily available.

# YUCATÁN FISH TACOS
## *Tacos de Pescado Tikin Xic*

*Tikin Xic*, pronounced "teekeen sheek," means dry fish. This dish originated in Isla Mujeres in the Yucatán Peninsula. Typically, a whitefish, or *mojarra*, is butterflied and seasoned with achiote paste mixed with bitter orange, garlic, and a dry rub, and then grilled with a direct flame or baked inside banana leaves.

2 ounces (a small square) achiote annatto paste

⅓ cup freshly squeezed orange juice

¼ white onion, coarsely chopped

1 tablespoon apple cider vinegar

3 garlic cloves, peeled

1 teaspoon dried Mexican oregano

6 whole black peppercorns

¼ cinnamon stick

2 whole cloves

1 teaspoon salt

1 large banana leaf

2 pounds red snapper, whole and butterflied

1 tomato, cut into ¼-inch slices

½ green bell pepper, seeded and cut into ¼-inch slices

¼ red onion, cut into ¼-inch slices

1 tablespoon corn oil

12 (6-inch) corn tortillas, warmed

1 cup Habanero Red Onion Salsa (page 102)

1. Preheat the oven to 450°F.

2. Put the achiote, orange juice, onion, apple cider vinegar, garlic, oregano, peppercorns, cinnamon stick, cloves, and salt in a blender. Blend on high until it becomes a smooth puree. Pour this adobo sauce into a small bowl and set it aside.

3. Line a baking sheet with a large piece of aluminum foil and place the banana leaf on top. Place the fish on the leaf flesh-side up. Use a brush to apply the achiote-adobo sauce to the fish, covering all the flesh.

4. Add slices of tomato, bell pepper, and red onion and drizzle with the oil.

5. Bake for 20 minutes until browned, and the fish flakes easily with a fork.

6. Serve the fish family style, including warm tortillas and the salsa. Allow your family or guests to make tacos their way.

**TIP:** Request that the fishmonger butterfly the fish. Use frozen banana leaves if fresh are not available or replace them with aluminum foil.

# BLACKENED SALMON TACOS WITH PASILLA PEPPERS
## *Tacos de Salmón en Chile Pasilla*

Salmon is perfect for grilling as it is fatty and moist. My favorite is sockeye salmon; it has a bright red color, is full of flavor, and allows the pasilla adobo to complement and not overwhelm the fish's flavor.

½ cup hot water

3 dried pasilla peppers, stemmed and seeded

2 garlic cloves, peeled

1 tablespoon chicken bouillon powder

1 teaspoon dried Mexican oregano

½ teaspoon freshly ground black pepper

2 pounds or 4 (8-ounce) skin-on sockeye salmon fillets

1 teaspoon corn oil

12 (6-inch) corn tortillas

**GARNISHES**

½ cup chopped fresh cilantro

½ cup Drunken Salsa (page 99)

2 limes, quartered

1. Pour the hot water into a medium bowl and submerge the pasilla peppers for about 10 minutes until softened.

2. Transfer the peppers to a blender with ½ cup of the soaking water. Add the garlic, chicken bouillon, oregano, and pepper. Blend on high until a smooth pepper paste forms. Pour the paste into a medium bowl and set it aside.

3. Place the salmon fillets on a chopping block or a plate, and use a brush to cover the salmon with the pasilla pepper paste.

4. Warm a large cast-iron grilling pan over high heat for about 3 minutes. Add the corn oil and tilt the skillet to coat it well.

5. Add the salmon to the skillet skin-side up. Cook until grilling marks show, about 4 minutes. Flip the salmon and lower the heat to medium. Sear for 3 to 4 minutes, until cooked through, then set the salmon on a plate.

6. Flake the cooked salmon with two forks. Place 2 to 3 tablespoons of the grilled fish in the middle of each tortilla and fold. Garnish with the cilantro, the salsa, and a few drops of lime juice and serve.

**¡SALUD!:** Pair with Classic Lime Margaritas (page 117).

# CHIPOTLE SHRIMP TACOS
## *Tacos de Camarón al Chipotle*

The spicy, buttery chipotle shrimp tacos are the best option for a taco bar party. This recipe is simple and so flavorful. The shrimp comes out juicy and meaty, with the perfect amount of zest and freshness from the lime cabbage slaw.

**FOR THE PURPLE-CABBAGE SLAW**

1 cup thinly sliced purple cabbage

3 tablespoons chopped fresh cilantro

Juice of 2 limes

½ teaspoon salt

½ teaspoon freshly ground black pepper

**FOR THE SHRIMP**

2 canned chipotle peppers en adobo, stemmed and seeded

1 tablespoon canned chipotle adobo sauce

1 teaspoon chicken bouillon powder

1 teaspoon garlic powder

½ teaspoon ground cumin

1 pound shrimp, peeled and deveined

2 tablespoons unsalted butter

12 (6-inch) corn or flour tortillas, warmed

**GARNISH**

1 cup Taquero-Style Non-Avocado Guacamole Salsa (page 97)

**TO MAKE THE PURPLE-CABBAGE SLAW**

1. In a mixing bowl, toss the cabbage and cilantro.

2. Dress with lime juice, salt, and pepper.

3. Mix, cover, and refrigerate until ready to use.

**TO MAKE THE SHRIMP**

4. Put the chipotle peppers and the adobo sauce in a blender or a food processor. Blend until everything becomes a smooth sauce. Pour this sauce into a bowl. Add the chicken bouillon, garlic powder, and cumin, and whisk.

5. Pat the shrimp dry with a paper towel to remove any water. Submerge the shrimp in the chipotle sauce and set them aside.

6. In a large sauté pan, heat the butter at medium-high heat for 1 to 2 minutes until bubbling.

7. Add the shrimp and sauté for 2 to 3 minutes on each side until they turn pink. Remove from the heat and set them aside.

8. Place 3 shrimp in the middle of each tortilla and fold. Garnish with the cabbage slaw and salsa and serve.

¡SALUD!: Pair with The Hidalgo (page 107).

# GRILLED TUNA TACOS
## *Tacos de Atún à la Parrilla*

Fresh tuna is a delight. The flavor is mild but luxurious. The texture is meaty, satisfying, and perfect for serving inside a taco. Typically, fresh tuna is a staple in Asian cuisine. However, the ingredient is versatile and pairs well with Mexican spices.

1 teaspoon ground cumin

1 teaspoon garlic powder

1 teaspoon salt

1 teaspoon freshly ground
black pepper

2 (1-inch-thick) tuna steaks

1 tablespoon corn oil

12 (6-inch) corn tortillas, warmed

**GARNISHES**

6 radishes, thinly sliced

½ cup chopped scallions, both
green and white parts

2 limes, quartered

½ cup Street Taco Salsa (page 98)

1. In a small bowl, combine the cumin, garlic powder, salt, and pepper and mix.

2. Drizzle the tuna steaks with corn oil on both sides and season with the spice mix on both sides.

3. Warm a large cast-iron grilling pan at high heat for 3 to 5 minutes. It must be hot.

4. Grill the tuna steaks for 2 minutes on each side. The center should be raw, and the steak must have the characteristic grilling marks. Allow the steaks to rest for 5 minutes before slicing.

5. Slice the tuna, place 3 slices in the middle of each tortilla, and fold. Garnish with the radishes and scallions and drizzle with lime juice. Finish by adding a teaspoon of salsa and serve.

**TIP:** Avoid cooking longer than the time specified. Overcooking the tuna will result in a tough and dry fish.

**¡SALUD!:** Pair with Mango Mezcal Mojitos (page 106).

# MAHI TACOS
## *Tacos de Pescado Mahi o Dorado*

One of my favorite things is Mahi, also known as a Dorado. This fish is white, flaky, and great for grilling. Those picky eaters that do not like fish will love these grilled Mahi tacos because the flavor is mild and delicious. The recipe is suitable for fresh or frozen fish.

¼ cup corn oil

1 teaspoon ground cumin

1 teaspoon dried thyme

1 teaspoon garlic powder

1 teaspoon hot paprika

1 teaspoon salt

½ teaspoon freshly ground black pepper

4 (4-ounce) Mahi fillets

Juice of 1 lime

8 (6-inch) corn tortillas, warmed

**GARNISHES**

12 avocado slices

½ cup Raw Green Salsa (page 94)

1. Pour the corn oil into a medium bowl. Add the cumin, thyme, garlic powder, hot paprika, salt, and pepper, and whisk.

2. Pat the Mahi fillets dry with a paper towel and brush the fillets on both sides with the spiced oil mix.

3. Warm a large cast-iron grilling pan at high heat for 3 to 5 minutes until hot.

4. Grill the fillets for 4 minutes on each side. The grilling marks must be well defined.

5. Remove the fish from the skillet to a plate. Allow it to rest for 3 minutes before flaking. Flake the fish with two forks and drizzle with the lime juice.

6. Place 2 to 3 tablespoons of the flaked fish in the middle of each tortilla and fold. Garnish with the avocado slices and salsa and serve.

**TRIVIA:** The birth of the fish taco happened in Baja, California.

# MEXICAN CRAB TACOS
## *Tacos de Jaiba*

*Jaiba* is the name in Spanish for crab. In Mexico, this crustacean is famous and consumed in guisados, soups (*chilpachole*), ceviche, salads (*salpicones*), seafood cocktails, stuffed, and inside small bites (*antojitos*). Garnish with six cups of Spicy Tomato Broth for Tacos (page 93), and one half cup of Peanut-Arbol Salsa (page 91).

**FOR THE CRAB**
2 cups water
1 tablespoon salt
1 pound wild-caught frozen, cooked Dungeness crab legs

**FOR THE CARROT-CABBAGE SLAW**
1 cup finely sliced green cabbage
½ cup shredded carrot
Juice of 2 limes
1 teaspoon salt

**FOR THE CRAB TACOS**
2 tablespoons unsalted butter
1 cup finely chopped white onion
3 garlic cloves, minced
1 green bell pepper, seeded and finely chopped
1 tablespoon chicken bouillon powder
Salt
Freshly ground black pepper
Juice of 1 lime
3 tablespoons chopped fresh cilantro
12 (6-inch) corn tortillas, warmed
1 cup corn oil

**TO MAKE THE CRAB**

1. Pour the water into a large soup pot, add the salt, and stir. Bring to a boil over medium-high heat.

2. Add the crab, cover, and steam for 4 to 5 minutes. Remove the crab from the hot water to cool for 10 minutes.

3. Use a crab cracker to remove the crabmeat from inside the shell and the legs and break the meat into pieces. Set it aside.

**TO MAKE THE CARROT-CABBAGE SLAW**

4. In a medium bowl, toss the cabbage, carrot, lime juice, and salt. Set it aside.

**TO MAKE THE CRAB TACOS**

5. In a large sauté pan, heat the butter over medium-high heat for 1 to 2 minutes until bubbling.

6. Add the onion and the garlic, and cook for 2 minutes, until fragrant. Then add the bell pepper and the chicken bouillon and stir. Cook for another 2 minutes and add the reserved crab. Fold the ingredients together using a spoon. Taste and add salt and pepper as needed.

7. Turn off the heat, drizzle the crab mixture with the lime juice, add the cilantro, and mix. Set it aside and allow the crab guisado to cool for 10 minutes.

8. Place 1 or 2 tablespoons of the crab guisado in the middle of a warm tortilla and fold. Secure each with a wooden toothpick.

9. In a large, deep sauté pan or skillet, heat the corn oil over high heat for 3 minutes. Fry the tacos, two at a time, for 3 minutes on each side, or until golden brown. Place the tacos on a paper-towel-lined plate to remove the excess oil.

10. Serve the tacos in a shallow dish and ladle a good amount of the spicy broth on top. Garnish with the carrot-cabbage slaw and salsa and serve.

• • • • • • • • • • • • • • • • • • • • • • • • • • • • • • • • • • • • • • • • • • •

**TRIVIA:** Mexico and the United States both have a National Taco Day. Mexico celebrates tacos on March 31 and the United States on October 4.

• • • • • • • • • • • • • • • • • • • • • • • • • • • • • • • • • • • • • • • • • • •

# GRILLED OCTOPUS TACOS
## *Tacos de Pulpo à la Parrilla*

Octopus, a cephalopod mollusk, is consumed in states near the Gulf of Mexico and is also famous worldwide. Campeche and Yucatán octopus are prepared in many ways, from seafood cocktails and stews to fried and breaded to grilled in octopus tapas and tacos.

1 pound fresh octopus, cleaned, without the head and the ink
8 cups water
1 white onion, cut into chunks
1 tablespoon sea salt
6 whole black peppercorns
2 bay leaves
1 thyme sprig
1 large lemon, halved
¼ cup Peanut-Arbol Salsa (page 91)
12 (6-inch) corn tortillas or Red Corn Tortillas (page 88), warmed
1 large avocado, mashed (about 1 cup)

### GARNISHES
½ cup sesame seeds, toasted
½ cup Street Taco Salsa (page 98)
2 limes, quartered

**¡SALUD!:** Pair with a Chamoy Michelada (page 112).

1. Place the raw octopus on a chopping block and pound it with a wooden mallet. This action will help break the fibers and result in a tender cooked octopus.

2. Place the raw octopus into an Instant Pot and add the water, onion, salt, peppercorns, bay leaves, and thyme. Squeeze in the lemon juice and add the lemon, too. The peel adds a tasty floral note.

3. Close the lid and cook on high pressure for 15 minutes. When cooking is complete, let the pressure release naturally.

4. Remove the octopus and transfer it to a chopping block. Allow it to cool for 5 minutes. Brush the cooked octopus with the Peanut-Arbol Salsa and set it aside.

5. Heat a large cast-iron grilling pan over high heat for 3 to 5 minutes. It must be hot. Grill the octopus for 5 minutes on each side. Use tongs for easy handling and turning.

6. Chop the grilled octopus into small pieces and set it aside.

7. Place 1 teaspoon of avocado mash and 2 tablespoons of grilled octopus in the middle of each tortilla and fold. Garnish with the toasted sesame seeds, the salsa, and a few drops of lime juice.

## CHAPTER 5

# BEEF, PORK, AND MORE

◄ Orange Pork Tacos, page 75

# CLASSIC BIRRIA TACOS
## *Tacos de Birria Clásica*

Birria is a spicy, fatty lamb consommé. This seventeenth-century recipe originated in Atequiza, Jalisco, known as the world's birria capital. Pair the tacos with birria broth for dipping and garnish with onion, cilantro, lime juice, and salsa. Store leftover birria in an airtight container in the refrigerator for up to three days.

**FOR THE BIRRIA**

1 pound lamb spareribs or loin chops, cut into 5-inch chunks

1 pound boneless lamb shoulder, cut into 5-inch chunks

1 tablespoon ground cumin

1 tablespoon freshly ground black pepper

1 teaspoon coarse sea salt

1 tablespoon corn oil

2 ancho chiles, stemmed and seeded

3 guajillo chiles, stemmed and seeded

2 chiles de árbol, stemmed and seeded (optional)

1 small onion, cut into chunks

3 garlic cloves, peeled

3 large Roma tomatoes, halved

4 whole allspice berries

3 whole cloves

1 cinnamon stick or 1 teaspoon ground

1 teaspoon dried Mexican oregano

1 teaspoon dried marjoram

2 bay leaves

1 tablespoon beef bouillon powder

2 cups beef stock

4 cups water

3 carrots, peeled and cut into thick sticks

¼ cup apple cider vinegar

Salt

**FOR THE BIRRIA TACOS**

12 Red Corn Tortillas (page 88)

2 cups shredded Monterey Jack cheese

2 tablespoons corn oil

**GARNISHES**

1 cup finely chopped red onions

1 cup coarsely chopped fresh cilantro

3 limes, quartered

1 cup Peanut-Arbol Salsa (page 91)

### TO MAKE THE BIRRIA

1. In a large bowl, season the lamb spareribs and shoulder with cumin, pepper, and salt.

2. Select the Sauté mode on an Instant Pot and heat the oil. Quick-fry the ancho, guajillo, and chiles de árbol (if using) for 3 minutes, until fragrant. Remove and set them aside.

3. Put in the onion and garlic and sauté for 2 minutes until softened. Add the tomatoes, allspice, cloves, cinnamon, oregano, marjoram, bay leaves, and bouillon. Cook for 7 minutes, until the tomatoes become soft.

4. Add the fried chiles and stock and simmer for another 15 minutes, or until the chiles are soft. Remove and set aside the bay leaves, allspice, and cinnamon stick.

5. Transfer the mixture to a blender and blend into a sauce. Strain and return it to the pot. Return the bay leaves, cinnamon, and allspice to the pot. Add the water, lamb, carrots, and apple cider vinegar.

6. Close the lid and cook on high pressure for 30 to 45 minutes. When cooking is complete, allow the pressure to release naturally. Carefully remove the lid and shred the meat using two forks. Season with salt. Strain the broth from the meat, reserving 6 cups in a large bowl.

### TO MAKE THE BIRRIA TACOS

7. Submerge the tortillas in the birria broth, stuff them with the cheese and meat, and fold.

8. In a large sauté pan or skillet, heat the oil over medium-high heat. Fry the tortillas, two at a time, for 2 minutes on each side, until the cheese melts. Garnish with red onions, cilantro, a squeeze of lime, and salsa and serve.

# POISONED TACOS
## *Tacos Envenenados*

The urban legend says these tacos were made famous by Don Lauro, a taquería owner in Zacatecas.

**FOR THE POISONED SAUCE**
1 tablespoon corn oil
1 medium white onion, sliced
2 garlic cloves, peeled
2 serrano peppers, stemmed
3 guajillo peppers, stemmed, seeded, and soaked for 15 minutes in boiling water
¼ cup warm water
1 tablespoon chicken bouillon powder

**FOR THE SPICY STUFFING**
½ cup crumbled Mexican chorizo
2 medium Yukon Gold potatoes, cooked, peeled, and mashed
1 cup Pinto Beans Two Ways (page 100)
Salt

**FOR THE TACOS**
2 cups shredded Monterey Jack cheese
12 (6-inch) corn tortillas, warmed
½ cup corn oil
1 cup Tomato-Serrano Salsa (page 89)

**TO MAKE THE POISONED SAUCE**

1. In a sauté pan, heat the corn oil over medium heat. Sauté the onion with the garlic and the serrano peppers for 2 minutes, until fragrant. Add the soaked guajillo peppers and cook for 1 minute.

2. In a blender, blend these ingredients with the warm water and chicken bouillon. Set it aside.

**TO MAKE THE SPICY STUFFING**

3. In a large sauté pan, put the chorizo and cook over medium heat for 4 minutes until crumbled.

4. Add the potatoes, pinto beans, and the poisoned sauce and stir. Season with salt if needed. Cook for 10 minutes over medium-low heat, occasionally stirring until the mixture becomes thick.

**TO MAKE THE TACOS**

5. Spoon 2 tablespoons of spicy stuffing and 1 tablespoon of cheese into each tortilla and fold.

6. In a large sauté pan or skillet, heat the oil over medium-high heat. Fry the tacos, one at a time, for 2 minutes on each side or until golden brown. Place on a paper-towel-lined plate to remove the excess oil.

7. Garnish with the salsa and serve. Store leftover stuffing and poisoned sauce in an airtight container in the refrigerator for up to 3 days.

# BEEF SKIRT TACOS
## *Tacos de Carne Deshebrada*

The beef skirt guisado is the ultimate homestyle dish to feed the family without breaking the bank. This recipe's components create other dishes such as soups, stews, and stuffed flautas and make Mexican beef skirt tacos.

**FOR THE BEEF SKIRT**

1 pound beef skirt steak

4 cups beef broth

2 cups water

1 onion, quartered

3 garlic cloves, peeled

1 tablespoon sea salt

6 whole black peppercorns

2 bay leaves

**FOR THE BEEF SKIRT TACOS**

2 tablespoons corn oil

1 cup finely chopped white onion

2 garlic cloves, chopped

1 large jalapeño, chopped

4 Roma tomatoes, diced

3 tablespoons beef broth

1 tablespoon beef
   bouillon powder

Salt

Freshly ground black pepper

12 (6-inch) corn or flour
   tortillas, warmed

**TIP:** Use 1 (28-ounce) can peeled plum tomatoes instead of fresh Roma tomatoes. For a spicier option, add 1 finely chopped serrano.

**TO MAKE THE BEEF SKIRT**

1. In an Instant Pot, combine the skirt steak, beef broth, water, onion, garlic, salt, peppercorns, and bay leaves.

2. Close the lid and cook on high pressure for 30 minutes. When cooking is complete, allow the pressure to release naturally.

3. Carefully open the lid and remove the meat. Shred the meat while still warm using two forks and then set aside.

**TO MAKE THE BEEF SKIRT TACOS**

4. In a sauté pan, heat the oil over medium-high heat for 2 minutes and sauté the onion and the garlic for 1 minute. Then add the jalapeño and cook for another minute.

5. Incorporate the shredded beef and mix. Add the tomatoes and season with the beef broth, the bouillon, and salt and pepper to taste, and cover.

6. Lower the heat to medium and allow the guisado to simmer for 5 minutes, until the flavors develop.

7. Spoon 2 to 3 tablespoons of shredded beef into the middle of each tortilla and fold. Pair the tacos with a bowl of Mexican Red Rice (page 95). Store leftover beef in an airtight container in the refrigerator for up to 3 days.

# BEEF PICADILLO TACOS
## *Tacos de Picadillo de Res*

The word *picadillo* means chopped meat. This guisado has been prepared for generations as part of our Spanish heritage. In Mexico, picadillo can include potatoes and roasted peppers or vegetables.

2 tablespoons corn oil

1 cup finely chopped white onion

2 garlic cloves, minced

1 pound ground beef, preferably lean sirloin

3 tablespoons beef broth or water

2 tablespoons tomato paste

1 tablespoon beef bouillon powder

2 cups frozen carrot and pea mix

Salt

Freshly ground black pepper

12 (6-inch) corn tortillas, warmed

½ cup corn oil

### GARNISHES

8 radishes, thinly sliced

3 cups shredded lettuce

½ cup Street Taco Salsa (page 98)

1. In a large sauté pan, heat the oil over medium-high heat for 1 to 2 minutes. Add the onion and the garlic, cook for 2 minutes, and then add the ground beef. Stir and cook for 3 minutes. Add the beef broth, tomato paste, and beef bouillon, and stir. Cook for another 3 minutes and add the frozen carrots and peas.

2. Cover and simmer the guisado over medium heat for 5 minutes, until the flavors develop. Taste and add salt and pepper as needed. Allow the picadillo to cool for 15 minutes before stuffing the tacos.

3. Spoon 2 tablespoons of picadillo into the middle of each tortilla and fold or roll.

4. In a large sauté pan or skillet, heat the oil over high heat for 3 minutes. Fry the tacos, one or two at a time, for 3 minutes on each side or until golden brown.

5. Place the tacos on a paper-towel-lined plate to remove the excess oil. Garnish the tacos with the radishes, lettuce, and salsa. Store leftover picadillo in an airtight container in the refrigerator for up to 3 days.

**TIP:** Prepare the picadillo the night before and store it inside the refrigerator in an airtight container.

# BEEF ASADA TACOS
## *Tacos de Carne Asada*

Beef grilled tacos originate in the North of Mexico, where parrilladas rule. It is common to marinate the bistecs (thin steaks) with beer and spices. These tacos have transcended frontiers and are famous worldwide.

¼ cup freshly squeezed lime juice

3 garlic cloves, minced

1 tablespoon seasoning sauce (Jugo Maggi) or soy sauce

4 (4-ounce) thin top sirloin steaks

1 teaspoon salt

1 teaspoon freshly ground black pepper

1 tablespoon corn oil

12 (6-inch) corn tortillas, warmed

**GARNISHES**

1 cup chopped white onion

½ cup coarsely chopped fresh cilantro

½ cup Street Taco Salsa (page 98)

1 lime, cut into wedges

1. In a large bowl, combine the lime juice, garlic, and seasoning sauce. Whisk the ingredients together. Add the steaks to the dressing, flip to coat both sides, and let the steaks rest, covered, for 30 minutes in the refrigerator.

2. In a small bowl, mix the salt and pepper and set it aside. Remove the steaks from the marinade and pat them dry with paper towels. Season with the salt and pepper and let the steaks rest in a dry container with a lid at room temperature for 10 minutes before grilling.

3. Warm a large cast-iron grilling pan over high heat for 3 minutes. Add the oil and tilt the pan to coat it well.

4. Add the steaks to the pan and cook for 3 minutes per side. The grilling marks must be well defined. Remove from the pan and let rest for 3 minutes before slicing.

5. Slice the steaks into strips. Place 2 to 3 strips in the middle of each tortilla and fold. Garnish with the onion, cilantro, salsa, and lime juice. Store leftover guisado in the refrigerator for up to 3 days.

**¡SALUD!:** Pair with the Chamoy Michelada (page 112).

# LEAN CARNITAS TACOS
## *Tacos de Carnitas Sin Grasa*

Carnitas are a traditional dish that originated right after the conquest. Hernán Cortés hosted the first pork feast, transforming Mexican cuisine into what it is today. This carnitas recipe is a modern twist on the classic Michoacán style fried in copper pots with generous amounts of lard.

2 teaspoons ground cumin

2 teaspoons dried Mexican oregano

1 teaspoon freshly ground black pepper

1 teaspoon chicken bouillon powder

1 pound pork loin, cut into 3-inch chunks

1 tablespoon corn oil

3 garlic cloves, peeled

1 cup water

12 (6-inch) corn tortillas, warmed

### GARNISHES

1 cup chopped white onion

½ cup cilantro leaves

1 cup Taquero-Style Non-Avocado Guacamole Salsa (page 97)

1. In a small bowl, mix the cumin, oregano, pepper, and chicken bouillon. Season the pork with this spice mix.

2. Pour the oil into an Instant Pot and select the Sauté mode. When hot, sear the pork loin for 2 minutes on each side. Use tongs to turn the meat easily.

3. Place the garlic cloves in a blender with the water, and blend. Add this garlic water on top of the pork.

4. Close the lid and cook on high pressure for 45 minutes. When cooking is complete, allow the pressure to release naturally. Carefully remove the lid and shred the pork using two forks.

5. Add 2 to 3 tablespoons of carnitas into the middle of each tortilla and fold. Garnish with the onion, cilantro, and a generous amount of salsa. Store leftover pork in an airtight container in the refrigerator for up to 3 days.

**TRIVIA:** Although there is much debate about the origin of Taco Tuesday, the phrase itself has been a registered trademark of the popular restaurant chain Taco John's since 1989.

# PORK AND BEANS MINER TACOS
## *Tacos Mineros de Cerdo con Frijoles*

Tacos mineros date to when mining was one of the essential industries in Mexico. But the so-called tacos were filled with gunpowder and wrapped with paper sheets to extract the precious metal. However, miners' wives fed them with another kind of miner tacos made with beans and pork meat later on—a staple in the mining states of Guanajuato, Hidalgo, and Zacatecas.

4 thick, smoked bacon slices, chopped

8 ounces ground pork

1 tablespoon salt

1 teaspoon dried thyme

1 tablespoon tomato paste

2 medium potatoes, cooked, peeled, and mashed

1 cup Pinto Beans Two Ways (page 100)

12 (6-inch) corn tortillas

½ cup corn oil

### GARNISHES

6 cups Spicy Tomato Broth for Tacos (page 93)

**TIP:** Authentic tacos traditionally use corn or flour tortillas, but there are many newer tortilla substitutes available in most grocery stores to consider if you have gluten or grain allergies. Try tortillas made from cauliflower, cheese, cactus, eggs, jicama, or almond flour.

1. In a large sauté pan or skillet, fry the bacon over medium-high heat for 2 minutes until crispy. Remove some of the bacon fat if desired.

2. Add the ground pork and cook for 2 to 3 minutes over medium heat.

3. Season the meat with the salt and thyme and add the tomato paste. Stir and continue cooking for 2 minutes more.

4. Add the mashed potatoes and the pinto beans and stir to combine. The mixture must be thick. Allow it to cool at room temperature for 15 minutes.

5. Spoon 2 to 3 tablespoons of pork stuffing into each tortilla and fold. Secure with a wooden toothpick if needed.

6. In a large sauté pan or skillet, heat the oil over medium-high heat and fry the tacos, one at a time, for 3 minutes on each side, or until golden brown. Place the tacos on a paper-towel-lined plate to remove excess oil.

7. Serve the tacos on a shallow plate with the spicy tomato broth. Store leftover pork in an airtight container in the refrigerator for up to 3 days.

# SHREDDED PORK PIBIL TACOS
## *Tacos de Cerdo Pibil*

The shredded pork pibil tacos are a typical Yucatán dish whose tradition dates back to pre-Hispanic times. The Spanish name is *cochinita*, meaning small pig. The traditional recipe uses an annatto paste marinade with citrus and spices and is then wrapped in banana leaves and baked inside a Mayan pib (an oven made with dirt and covered with hot stones), but we are using the Instant Pot to save time.

1½ cups freshly squeezed orange juice

1 small white onion, cut into 1-inch chunks

½ cup apple cider vinegar

1 (3½-ounce) package achiote annatto paste

3 garlic cloves, peeled

1 teaspoon chicken bouillon powder

1 tablespoon pork lard or corn oil

1 pound pork loin, cut into 4-inch pieces

12 (6-inch) corn tortillas, warmed

**GARNISH**

1 cup Habanero Red Onion Salsa (page 102)

1. Place the orange juice, onion, apple cider vinegar, achiote, garlic, and chicken bouillon in a blender. Blend on high for 2 to 3 minutes until smooth.

2. Place the lard into an Instant Pot and select the Sauté mode. Heat the lard for 3 minutes, and then sear the pork chunks for 2 minutes, using tongs to turn the meat, until browned. Pour in the achiote sauce and mix it with the pork meat.

3. Close the lid and cook on high pressure for 45 minutes. When cooking is complete, let the pressure release naturally.

4. Carefully open the lid and shred the pork using two forks.

5. Spoon 2 to 3 tablespoons of the pork pibil into the middle of each tortilla and fold. Garnish with the salsa and serve. Store leftover pork in an airtight container in the refrigerator for up to 3 days.

**TRIVIA:** Americans eat a whopping 4.5 billion tacos a year. This is understandable because tacos rule!

# ORANGE PORK TACOS
## *Tacos de Cerdo à la Naranja*

Sweet-and-sour flavors are common in Mexican cuisine. Pork is an excellent meat to create an Asian-inspired dish and make tacos Mexican style.

**FOR THE CARROT-CUCUMBER SLAW**

3 carrots, shredded

1 English cucumber, shredded

Juice of 2 limes

1 teaspoon Tajin seasoning

**FOR THE ORANGE PORK TACOS**

1 cup ketchup

1 cup freshly squeezed orange juice

1 cup tomato juice

3 tablespoons chipotle sauce

1 tablespoon seasoning sauce (Jugo Maggi) or soy sauce

1 teaspoon ground cumin

1 teaspoon garlic powder

1 teaspoon freshly ground black pepper

1 teaspoon salt

1 pound pork shoulder, cut into 2-inch pieces

1 tablespoon corn oil

12 (6-inch) flour tortillas, warmed

3 tablespoons toasted sesame seeds

**TO MAKE THE CARROT-CUCUMBER SLAW**

1. In a medium salad bowl, combine the carrots and cucumber. Dress with the lime juice and Tajin seasoning. Stir and set it aside.

**TO MAKE THE ORANGE PORK TACOS**

2. In a medium bowl, combine the ketchup, orange juice, tomato juice, chipotle sauce, and seasoning sauce and whisk. Set it aside.

3. In a small bowl, combine the cumin, garlic powder, pepper, and salt and mix. Season the pork with this spice mix.

4. Pour the oil into an Instant Pot and select the Sauté mode. Heat the oil for 2 minutes, until shimmering, then sear the pork chunks for 3 minutes, turning using tongs, until lightly browned. Pour in the orange sauce and stir to coat all the meat evenly.

5. Close the lid and cook on high pressure for 45 minutes. When cooking is complete, let the pressure release naturally. Carefully open the lid and shred the pork using two forks.

6. Spoon 2 to 3 tablespoons of the pork into the middle of each tortilla and fold. Garnish with the slaw and sesame seeds. Store leftover pork in an airtight container in the refrigerator for up to 3 days.

# BEER VEAL CUTLETS TACOS
## *Tacos de Ternera à la Cerveza*

Veal is a common protein in Mexican cuisine. We enjoy it grilled and dressed in simple ingredients. The taste of veal is mild, so this meat goes well with almost everything and doesn't have a beefy flavor—a good alternative for the picky eaters at home.

4 (4-ounce) veal cutlets

1 cup blond beer

1 tablespoon beef bouillon powder

1 teaspoon freshly ground black pepper

1 tablespoon corn oil

Juice of 1 lime

8 (6-inch) corn tortillas, warmed

**GARNISH**

½ cup Street Taco Salsa (page 98)

1. Place the veal cutlets in a large bowl, pour the beer on top, cover, and marinate for 15 minutes in the refrigerator.

2. In a small bowl, mix the beef bouillon and pepper. Remove the veal cutlets from the beer marinade and pat them dry with paper towels. Season with the bouillon mixture and place the veal in a dry container at room temperature for 5 minutes to rest before grilling.

3. Warm a large cast-iron grilling pan over high heat for 3 minutes. Put in the oil and tilt the pan to coat it well.

4. Add the veal cutlets to the pan and cook for 2 minutes per side. The grilling marks must be well defined. Remove from the pan and allow the meat to rest for 2 minutes. Chop the veal into small pieces, place it in a bowl, and drizzle it with the lime juice.

5. Place 2 tablespoons of the grilled veal into the middle of each tortilla, garnish with the salsa, and serve.

**TIP:** It is essential to pat the veal dry before grilling for well-defined grilling marks.

# THIN STEAK MEXICAN TACOS
## *Tacos de Bistec à la Mexicana*

The thin steak Mexican stew for tacos is a popular recipe for tacos acorazados or tacos de guisado—a staple of the state of Morelos and a standard offering among street taco vendors and taco eateries in Mexico City. Serve these tacos with a side of Pinto Beans Two Ways (page 100).

1 tablespoon corn oil

1 cup finely chopped onion

2 garlic cloves, minced

4 (4-ounce) thin sirloin steaks, cut into strips

3 Roma tomatoes, diced

½ cup beef broth or water

2 jalapeño peppers, chopped

2 tablespoons tomato paste

1 tablespoon beef bouillon powder

½ teaspoon freshly ground black pepper

12 (6-inch) corn or flour tortillas

1. In a large sauté pan or skillet, warm the oil over medium-high heat for 2 minutes. Sauté the onion with the garlic for 1 minute, until fragrant, and then add the sirloin steak strips.

2. Cook the beef for 2 minutes, constantly stirring, until browned. Add the tomatoes, beef broth, jalapeño peppers, tomato paste, beef bouillon, and pepper.

3. Stir and mix all ingredients. Lower the heat to medium, cover, and cook for 7 minutes, or until the liquid reduces. Set it aside and keep covered.

4. Spoon 2 tablespoons of the steak guisado into the middle of each tortilla. Fold and serve.

**TIP:** Use steak tips instead of thin sirloin steaks. Make quesatacos by adding shredded cheese or incorporating Mexican Melted Cheese with Chorizo (page 90) as a side.

**¡SALUD!:** Pair with the Mango-Lime Agua Fresca (page 109).

# CHAMOY PORK RIBS TACOS
## *Tacos de Costilla de Cerdo al Chamoy*

Chamoy-barbecue glaze is a trendy option and happens to be perfect for making chamoy pork rib tacos. Chamoy is a sweet, spicy, and sour sauce used to craft sweets and drinks. But it is so versatile that it can be used for dressing white meats and goes perfect with pork. This pork ribs recipe is simple and suitable for taco parties at home.

**FOR THE CARROT-CABBAGE SLAW**
2 carrots, shredded
1 cup shredded green cabbage
Juice of 1 lime
1 teaspoon Tajin seasoning or salt

**FOR THE PORK RIBS**
1 (1-pound) rack baby back pork ribs
1 cup Tamarind Sauce "Chamoy" (page 96)
Nonstick cooking spray
1 teaspoon freshly ground black pepper
12 (6-inch) corn or flour tortillas

**GARNISH**
½ cup Peanut-Arbol Salsa (page 91)

**TO MAKE THE CARROT-CABBAGE SLAW**

1. In a medium bowl, combine the carrots and cabbage.

2. Dress with the lime juice and Tajin seasoning. Stir and set it aside.

**TO MAKE THE PORK RIBS**

3. Preheat the oven to 375°F.

4. Prepare the ribs by removing the membrane on the back. Using a sharp knife, cut the ribs apart and set them aside.

5. In a large bowl, combine the chamoy sauce and the ribs. Make sure to drench the ribs in the sauce.

6. Spray a large baking sheet with nonstick cooking spray and spread the ribs evenly on the sheet, leaving space between each rib.

7. Sprinkle the ribs with the pepper and cover with aluminum foil—but do not close completely.

8. Bake the ribs for 1 hour, turning every 15 to 20 minutes. Remove the foil and finish by broiling at 500°F for 3 to 5 minutes, until browned.

9. Serve the ribs inside the tortillas. Garnish with the carrot-cabbage slaw and the salsa. Store leftover pork in an airtight container in the refrigerator for up to 3 days.

# CAMPECHANO TACOS
## *Tacos Campechanos*

These tacos are famous in Querétaro and have a mix of lean and fatty meats. These tacos can include chicharrones, chorizo, or bacon combined with shredded or grilled beef, pork, or chicken. These tacos are the best way to create a taco meal using leftovers while saving time and money.

1 pound skirt steak
1 teaspoon garlic powder
1 teaspoon salt
½ teaspoon freshly ground
　black pepper
1 tablespoon corn oil
12 (6-inch) corn tortillas
1 cup cooked Mexican chorizo
　or bacon
1 cup pork cracklings

**GARNISHES**
1 cup chopped white onion
½ cup coarsely chopped cilantro
½ cup Street Taco Salsa (page 98)

**TIP:** You can make tacos campecha-nos with anything! Check for leftovers inside your refrigerator and create your new flavors and combinations. Just make sure to include different meats and textures.

**¡SALUD!:** Pair with the Piña Colada Agua Fresca (page 108).

1. Place the skirt steak on a chopping block and pound it with a meat tenderizer. This action will help break the fibers and result in a tender skirt steak. It is necessary to do this as this beef cut tends to be somewhat tough.

2. In a small bowl, mix the garlic powder, salt, and pepper. Use this seasoning to sprinkle the skirt steak on both sides.

3. Warm a large cast-iron grilling pan over high heat for 3 to 5 minutes until hot. Put in the oil and tilt the pan to coat it well.

4. Grill the skirt steak for 15 minutes, flipping it every 3 to 5 minutes. Use tongs for easy handling and turning.

5. Remove the skirt steak from the pan and let it rest for 3 minutes before slicing to keep the meat juices inside. Cut the skirt steak into thin strips and set aside.

6. In a comal or large nonstick skillet, heat the tortillas over medium heat for 30 to 45 seconds on each side, until soft and pliable, and transfer to a platter.

7. Place 3 strips of grilled skirt steak, 1 tablespoon of cooked chorizo, and 1 tablespoon of pork cracklings in the middle of each tortilla and fold. Garnish with the onion, cilantro, and salsa. Serve.

# PORK ADOBO TACOS
## *Tacos de Cerdo en Adobo*

The adobo sauce is part of the culinary heritage of Spain. In Mexico, this sauce results from a combination of dried peppers, and the color depends on the type of peppers used. There are many adobos, but the most popular one is guajillo and ancho peppers. Vinegar is a vital component of the adobo as it balances the flavors. Depending on the region, adobos could also include spices such as cinnamon and cloves. But do not confuse adobo with mole. The difference between the sauces is palpable, because adobo is not sweet and does not contain seeds.

**FOR THE ADOBO**

2 cups hot water

3 guajillo peppers, stemmed and seeded

2 ancho peppers, stemmed and seeded

1 cup amber beer

½ medium white onion, cut into chunks

3 garlic cloves, minced

2 tablespoons tomato paste

2 tablespoons apple cider vinegar

**FOR THE PORK**

1 tablespoon pork lard or corn oil

1 pound pork shoulder, cut into 2- to 3-inch chunks

1 tablespoon chicken bouillon powder

1 tablespoon dried Mexican oregano

½ teaspoon salt

½ teaspoon ground black pepper

12 (6-inch) corn or flour tortillas, warmed

**TO MAKE THE ADOBO**

1. In a saucepan, combine the hot water and the dried peppers and soak for 10 minutes, until soft.

2. Place the softened peppers, beer, onion, garlic, tomato paste, and apple cider vinegar in the blender.

3. Blend the ingredients for 2 to 3 minutes until you get a smooth sauce.

**TO MAKE THE PORK**

4. Place the lard into an Instant Pot and select the Sauté mode. Heat the lard for 3 minutes, then sear the pork chunks for 2 minutes, turning the meat using tongs, until lightly browned. Pour the adobo sauce and mix it with the pork. Season with the chicken bouillon, oregano, salt, and pepper and stir again.

5. Close the lid and cook on high pressure for 45 minutes. When cooking is complete, allow the pressure to release naturally.

6.  Spoon 2 to 3 tablespoons of pork adobo into the middle of each tortilla and fold. Store leftover pork in an airtight container in the refrigerator for up to 3 days.

•••••••••••••••••••••••••••••••••••••••••••••••••

**TIP:** Serve the pork adobo tacos with a side of Mexican Red Rice (page 95) and Pinto Beans Two Ways (page 100). Use a leaner cut of pork, such as pork loin, instead of pork shoulder. Garnish the tacos with fries (it sounds strange, but it is so yummy).

•••••••••••••••••••••••••••••••••••••••••••••••••

**¡SALUD!:** Pair with Oatmeal Horchata (page 110).

•••••••••••••••••••••••••••••••••••••••••••••••••

# TEQUILA LAMB TACOS
## *Tacos de Carnero al Tequila*

Lamb is a delightful cut of meat, but it requires time for cooking; that's why braising is the best method to achieve flavorful, tender meat. Cooking with tequila or mezcal is a fantastic way to add umami to meats and helps with tenderizing the lamb meat, too. These tacos are a great addition to a party menu or a special celebratory meal.

**FOR THE RUB**

1 tablespoon salt

1 teaspoon chile ancho powder

1 teaspoon chipotle powder

1 teaspoon ground cumin

1 teaspoon garlic powder

1 teaspoon dried mint

**FOR THE LAMB**

1 pound boneless lamb shoulder

1 tablespoon corn oil

2 cups water or chicken broth

½ cup tequila reposado

**FOR THE TACOS**

12 (6-inch) corn or flour tortillas, warmed

1 cup coarsely chopped fresh cilantro

2 limes, quartered

1 cup Drunken Salsa (page 99)

**TO MAKE THE RUB**

1. In a small bowl, combine the salt, ancho powder, chipotle powder, cumin, garlic powder, and mint. Whisk and set aside.

**TO MAKE THE LAMB**

2. Preheat the oven to 350°F.

3. Cut the lamb into 2- to 3-inch chunks and remove any fat. In a large bowl, season the lamb chunks with the spice rub, making sure to season each piece of meat.

4. In a Dutch oven, heat the oil over high heat for 2 minutes.

5. Sear the lamb for 4 minutes per side, until lightly browned. Lower the heat to medium and add the water and tequila.

6. Stir all ingredients together and cook the lamb for 1 hour, uncovered. Turn the lamb a couple of times throughout the braising process.

7. The tequila lamb is done when most of the liquid evaporates, and the meat is tender.

**TO MAKE THE TACOS**

**8.** Spoon 2 to 3 tablespoons of the tequila lamb into the center of each tortilla and fold. Garnish with the cilantro, lime juice, and salsa. Store leftover lamb in an airtight container in the refrigerator for up to 3 days.

• • • • • • • • • • • • • • • • • • • • • • • • • • • • • • • • • • • • • • • • •

**TIP:** Use lamb leg instead of the shoulder for a milder taste. I recommend the shoulder as it is less pricey and has a richer flavor that pairs well with the tequila and the spices.

• • • • • • • • • • • • • • • • • • • • • • • • • • • • • • • • • • • • • • • • •

**¡SALUD!:** Pair with The Hidalgo (page 107).

• • • • • • • • • • • • • • • • • • • • • • • • • • • • • • • • • • • • • • • • •

# LAMB BARBACOA TACOS
## *Tacos de Barbacoa de Cordero*

Barbacoa tacos is one of my family's favorite Sunday meals. The Instant Pot makes it easy to cook the lamb, resulting in tender meat that falls off the bone. The consommé is full of flavor, and the perfect side to serve for an authentic barbacoa experience. Make sure to have enough cilantro and onion, Peanut-Arbol Salsa, and limes in order to make the best barbacoa tacos at home!

1 tablespoon corn oil

2 tablespoons dried Mexican oregano

2 tablespoons ground cumin

1 tablespoon dried thyme

2 bay leaves

1 small onion, cut into chunks

1 pound lamb shoulder

½ garlic head

2 tablespoons guajillo powder or ancho chile

2 tablespoons beef bouillon powder

1 tablespoon hot paprika

½ teaspoon freshly ground black pepper

4 cups water

1 cup amber beer

2 tablespoons apple cider vinegar

12 (6-inch) corn or flour tortillas, warmed

**GARNISHES**

1 cup coarsely chopped fresh cilantro

1 cup chopped red onion

2 limes, quartered

½ cup Peanut-Arbol Salsa (page 91)

1. Pour the oil into an Instant Pot and select the Sauté mode. Heat the oil and sauté the oregano, cumin, thyme, and bay leaves. Add the onion and stir for 1 minute.

2. Chop the lamb into 4-inch pieces. Add the garlic and the lamb chunks. Continue sautéing and stirring. Turn off the Sauté mode and add the guajillo powder, beef bouillon, paprika, and pepper and mix well. Add the water, beer, and apple cider vinegar.

3. Close the lid and cook on high pressure for 1 hour and 30 minutes. When cooking is complete, allow the pressure to release naturally. Carefully remove the lid and shred the lamb using two forks.

4. Spoon 2 to 3 tablespoons of shredded barbacoa lamb into the middle of each tortilla and fold. Garnish with the cilantro, red onion, lime juice, and salsa. Serve the tacos with a side of the barbacoa broth. Store leftover lamb in an airtight container in the refrigerator for up to 3 days.

• • • • • • • • • • • • • • • • • • • • • • • • • • • • • • • • • • • • • • • •

**¡SALUD!:** Pair with the Chamoy Michelada (page 112) or your favorite Mexican beer.

• • • • • • • • • • • • • • • • • • • • • • • • • • • • • • • • • • • • • • • •

**TRIVIA:** According to one popular theory, barbacoa is believed to have originated centuries ago in Barbados and was later brought to Mexico.

• • • • • • • • • • • • • • • • • • • • • • • • • • • • • • • • • • • • • • • •

## CHAPTER 6

# TORTILLAS, SAUCES, AND MORE

# RED CORN TORTILLAS
## *Tortillas Rojas*

Popular in the northern region of Mexico, these vibrant corn tortillas are flavored with dried ancho and guajillo chiles. Traditionally, these tortillas are used to make enchiladas, quesadillas, and, of course, tacos, but my favorite way is to use them for making Classic Birria Tacos (page 66).

1½ cups chicken broth or water
1 dried ancho chile, stemmed and seeded
1 guajillo chile, stemmed and seeded
2 cups masa harina
1 teaspoon salt
1 cup warm water

**TIP:** Corn masa needs enough hydration, so cover it to maintain its moisture and dip your fingers in water when forming the masa balls. Making tortillas is an art and requires practice.

1. In a medium saucepan, bring the chicken broth and dried chiles to a boil over high heat. Remove from the heat. Cover the saucepan to allow the chiles to soften and let cool completely. Puree the chiles and broth in a blender until smooth.

2. Preheat a large nonstick skillet or comal over medium heat.

3. In a medium bowl, combine the masa harina and salt. Stir in the chile puree, mixing until the dough comes together and forms a ball. Add warm water as needed. (Be conservative when adding the water; masa cannot be watery. Masa needs to be like a Play-Doh consistency and moist.)

4. Divide the dough into 12 (1½-inch) balls. Using a tortilla press lined with two pieces of plastic wrap or parchment paper, flatten a ball of masa into a 6-inch circle. If you do not have a tortilla press, place a masa ball between two pieces of plastic wrap or parchment paper, and flatten with a large, heavy plate.

5. Cook the tortilla in a hot, dry skillet over medium heat for 45 seconds to 1 minute per side until fully cooked and the tortilla starts to fill with air. Remove from the heat and keep warm by covering it with a clean kitchen towel. Repeat with the remaining masa balls.

# TOMATO-SERRANO SALSA
## *Salsa de Tomate y Serrano*

This salsa is a must-have when eating tacos as it complements almost all proteins and is so simple to put together. The trick is to boil the peppers to where they are soft enough to create the perfect salsa consistency. I recommend roasting the ingredients on the stovetop over high heat using a skillet or a comal before boiling and adding ground cumin and a canned chipotle for extra flavor.

3 serrano peppers, stemmed

5 plum tomatoes or 1 (28-ounce) can peeled plum tomatoes, undrained

½ medium onion

3 garlic cloves, peeled

1 teaspoon salt

1 large handful fresh cilantro, including stems

1. Fill a soup pot with water and add the serrano peppers. Bring to a boil over medium heat and cook for 15 minutes or until the peppers turn a gray-green color and are soft.

2. Add the tomatoes to the pot and cook for another 5 minutes using the same boiling water until the peel wrinkles and it is easy to remove.

3. In a sauté pan or skillet, roast the onion and garlic on high heat for 2 to 3 minutes per side until browned.

4. Transfer the cooked peppers, tomatoes, onion, garlic, and salt to a blender, add ¼ cup of the boiling water, and then pulse to blend. Taste and season with additional salt, if needed.

5. Puree the salsa until thoroughly combined. Then add the cilantro and pulse to chop it coarsely.

6. Pour the salsa into a resealable airtight container and refrigerate until ready to serve, up to 2 days.

**TIP:** For perfectly peeled tomatoes, remove the stem and cut a shallow X on the bottom of the tomato before boiling. Add more serrano peppers to increase the heat level.

# MEXICAN MELTED CHEESE WITH CHORIZO
## *Queso Fundido con Chorizo "Choriqueso"*

Queso Fundido is a staple in Mexican taquerías, served as an appetizer, as a side dish for carne asada, or with tacos in general. It comes in small clay bowls and is cooked on the grill. Some melt the cheese directly on the skillet and use a spatula to serve it, and others bake it. No matter the technique, the richness of crumbled chorizo permeates the dish, resulting in a pitch-perfect filling for warm tortillas. Talk about a crowd-pleaser—after all, who doesn't love a vat of bubbly, gooey cheese?

Nonstick cooking spray
1 cup Mexican chorizo, casing removed
2 cups shredded Monterey Jack cheese
8 (6-inch) corn or flour tortillas, warmed

GARNISH
½ cup Tomato-Serrano Salsa (page 89)

1. Preheat the oven to 425°F. Spray a 3- to 4-cup ovenproof baking dish or a clay pan with cooking spray.

2. While the oven is heating, in a medium sauté pan or skillet, brown the chorizo for 8 to 10 minutes over medium heat, breaking it into bits until cooked. Drain and discard the remaining fat.

3. Add the chorizo evenly to the baking dish and top it with the cheese. Bake for 20 minutes, or until the cheese is melted, browned, and bubbly.

4. Spoon 2 to 3 tablespoons of the melted cheese with chorizo into the middle of each tortilla. Garnish with the salsa and fold.

TIP: The chorizo used for this recipe is Mexican style; it crumbles when cooked. Replace the chorizo with roasted poblanos, and the Monterey Jack cheese with Oaxaca, Menonita, Asadero, or Chihuahua.

# PEANUT-ARBOL SALSA
## *Salsa Macha de Cacahuate y Chile de Árbol*

The Salsa Macha dates from pre-Hispanic times. The original recipe first appeared in Veracruz and had peanuts, palm oil, chile morita, and comapeño. As time has passed, the sauce has transformed, and other ingredients have been added or replaced. *Macha* refers to people brave enough to consume such spicy salsa. The flavor notes are toasty, nutty, and smoky.

1 cup corn oil
6 garlic cloves, peeled
10 chiles de árbol, stemmed
10 morita chiles, stemmed
3 tablespoons sesame seeds
1 tablespoon salt, or more
 if needed
1 tablespoon apple cider vinegar
½ cup roasted, unsalted peanuts,
 finely chopped

1. In a large sauté pan or skillet, heat the oil over medium-high heat until shimmering. Add the garlic and cook for 2 minutes, then remove and set aside.

2. Turn off the heat and add the dried chiles. Fry them for a maximum of 1 to 2 minutes until fluffy, remove from the hot oil, and set aside.

3. In a small skillet, toast the sesame seeds for 2 to 3 minutes over medium heat. Remove and set them aside in a small bowl.

4. Transfer the garlic, the fried peppers, the salt, the vinegar, and the oil used for frying to a food processor or a blender. Blend for 1 to 2 minutes. Make sure the ingredients are at room temperature before blending.

5. Pour the salsa into a large mason jar and add the toasted sesame seeds and peanuts. Stir using a spoon for 1 minute. Enjoy immediately or refrigerate for up to 1 month.

TIP: For some variation, replace the peanuts with pepitas, almonds, or hazelnuts. Use pasilla and guajillo peppers instead of morita. And replace chile de árbol with Japanese red peppers.

# PICKLED JALAPEÑOS
## *Jalapeños en Escabeche*

Sure, the canned pickled jalapeños you buy at the supermarket are okay, but once you taste the fresh flavor of making them at home, you'll never go back to store-bought.

1 tablespoon corn oil
1 medium onion, sliced
4 garlic cloves, peeled
4 whole black peppercorns
1 teaspoon dried thyme
1 teaspoon dried
   Mexican oregano
2 bay leaves
6 jalapeños, sliced
3 medium carrots, sliced
1 tablespoon coarse salt
½ cup white vinegar
½ cup water

1. Sterilize 2 (16-ounce) mason jars, rings, and lids in boiling water for at least 15 minutes. Carefully remove them from the water to dry completely on top of a clean towel.

2. In a large sauté pan or skillet, heat the oil over medium-high heat. Add the onion, garlic, peppercorns, thyme, oregano, and bay leaves, and sauté, stirring, for 1 to 2 minutes.

3. Add the jalapeños and the carrots. Stir to combine and cook for 2 minutes. Add the salt, pour in the white vinegar and the water, and allow the veggies to simmer for 2 to 3 minutes to absorb the flavor of the brine and the aroma of the spices.

4. Ladle the pickled veggies into each of the jars and top off with brine to fill the jar. Leave between ¼- to ½-inch headspace from the liquid to the top of the jar. Cover with the lids.

5. Allow to cool and refrigerate for 24 hours before serving. The pickled jalapeños will keep fresh for several weeks when kept inside the refrigerator.

**TRIVIA:** Mexico holds the record for making the longest taco at a whopping 134 feet (40.9 meters)!

# SPICY TOMATO BROTH FOR TACOS
## *Caldillo Picante de Tomate para Tacos*

Broths are common when serving fried tacos (tacos dorados) or flautas. These add flavor and are comforting. Many enjoy dipping the tacos and spooning the consommé. It is like eating a complete meal in one single course.

1 cup hot water

1 guajillo pepper, stemmed and seeded

3 chile de árbol, stemmed

5 Roma tomatoes

½ white onion

3 garlic cloves, peeled

1 tablespoon corn oil

1 tablespoon chicken, beef, or vegetable bouillon powder

1 teaspoon ground cumin

1 teaspoon dried Mexican oregano

½ teaspoon freshly ground black pepper

5 cups chicken, beef, or vegetarian broth

Salt

1. Pour the hot water into a saucepan and submerge the guajillo and chile de árbol for 15 minutes until plumped and soft. Strain, reserving the soaking water.

2. In a sauté pan or skillet, roast the tomatoes, onion, and garlic over medium to high heat for 3 to 5 minutes, turning for an even roast. Peel the tomatoes and remove the cores. Halve the tomatoes, spoon out the seeds, and set them aside.

3. Transfer the softened peppers, roasted tomatoes, onion, garlic, and pepper-soaking water to a blender. Blend on high for 2 to 3 minutes until it becomes a smooth puree.

4. In a large soup pot, heat the oil over medium heat until shimmering and pour in the spicy tomato puree. Add the chicken bouillon, cumin, oregano, and pepper and cook it for 1 to 2 minutes until bubbling.

5. Pour the chicken broth into the mixture and stir. Cover and simmer the broth for 10 minutes, until the flavors meld. Taste and add salt if needed.

6. Refrigerate in an airtight container for up to 4 days or freeze for 6 months.

**TIP:** Use canned peeled plum tomatoes instead of fresh ones. Replace the chicken bouillon and broth with shrimp bouillon and seafood broth for seafood tacos.

# RAW GREEN SALSA
## *Salsa Verde Cruda*

There are many variations of salsa verde. Some use classic tomatillo, and others a smaller version called "miltomate," a green or purple tomatillo that bursts with flavor and is considered specialty produce. In Mexico City, Tlaxcala, Puebla, Hidalgo, and Michoacán, this salsa could be roasted, raw, or cooked, smooth or coarsely chopped (salsa martajada), and might include other herbs such as *quelite* (pigweed), queso fresco, and avocado chunks. No matter the technique, raw green salsa verde is a staple and pairs with almost every taco out there, especially Lean Carnitas Tacos (page 72).

6 tomatillos, husked and rinsed with water

½ cup fresh cilantro with stems

¼ small white onion or 2 tablespoons chopped onion

2 serrano peppers, or more, stemmed

1 garlic clove, peeled

2 tablespoons water, if needed

1 tablespoon salt

1. Place the tomatillos, cilantro, onion, serrano peppers, and garlic in a blender or food processor. Pulse the salsa for 2 minutes. Add 1 to 2 tablespoons of water as needed. The salsa should be chunky.

2. Season with salt and serve in a bowl. Store the salsa fresh in an airtight container in the refrigerator for up to 3 days.

**TIP:** Add as many peppers as you like. If serrano peppers are not available, use jalapeños. Add chopped avocado, onion, or queso fresco.

**TRIVIA:** Did you know the first taco truck originated in New York in 1966? It didn't have a full kitchen and was primarily used for catered events.

# MEXICAN RED RICE
## *Arroz Rojo Mexicano*

Mexican rice is a staple in Mexican cuisine and is prepared with many variations depending on the region. Some add diced potatoes, others incorporate peas and carrots, others use fresh tomatoes, and others canned. Mexican rice is called *arroz rojo* because it has a reddish color due to the typical Mexican tomato *sofrito*. This rice is not spicy even though it cooks with whole serrano peppers for additional flavor.

2 tablespoons corn oil

1 cup long-grain rice, rinsed and dried

2 serrano peppers, with stems on

2 garlic cloves, peeled

1 cup Mexican-style tomato sauce

1 tablespoon chicken bouillon powder

1 teaspoon salt

½ teaspoon freshly ground black pepper

2 cups warm water

1 handful fresh cilantro with stems

1 cup frozen peas and carrots

1. In a medium sauté pan or skillet, heat the oil over medium-high heat until shimmering.

2. Fry the rice for 5 to 7 minutes until toasty. Then add the serrano peppers and garlic, and sauté for 1 to 2 minutes.

3. Add the tomato sauce, stir, and season with the chicken bouillon, salt, and pepper.

4. Pour in the warm water, stir once, and add the cilantro. Lower the heat to medium, cover, and cook the rice for 15 minutes. Do not stir. If needed, add more warm water, but be conservative with it to avoid mushy rice.

5. Add the frozen peas and carrots, cover, and cook for another 5 minutes. Turn off the heat. Remove the cilantro and discard. Cover the rice and let sit. After 5 to 10 minutes, use a fork to fluff the rice and serve.

**TIP:** Rinse the rice inside a colander with running water until the water comes out clean. Doing this will prevent lumpy rice. For an authentic flavor, use El Pato canned tomato sauce.

# TAMARIND SAUCE "CHAMOY"
## *Chamoy de Tamarindo*

Chamoy is a sweet, savory, and spicy sauce used to craft candies, desserts, and beverages. Asian immigrants in the 1950s brought umeboshi plums (a cross between a plum and an apricot) to Mexico, which is how chamoy sauce first appeared. This sauce uses tamarind pods, hibiscus flowers, and piloncillo among other ingredients. All these ingredients are easily found on Amazon or at a Mexican market.

1 cup hot water
1 cup tamarind
1 cup dried apricots
1 cup granulated sugar
1 piloncillo cone, or ½ cup packed brown sugar
½ cup hibiscus flowers
5 dried prunes, pitted
3 guajillo peppers, stemmed
6 chiles de árbol, stemmed
⅓ cup apple cider vinegar
1 teaspoon pink salt
3 cups water
3 tablespoons Tajin seasoning
Juice of 1 lime

1. In a large saucepan, combine the hot water and tamarind for 15 minutes until soft, then you'll be able to easily remove the pits. Strain, reserving the soaking water.

2. In a large pot, combine the apricots, sugar, piloncillo, hibiscus flowers, prunes, guajillo peppers, chiles de árbol, apple cider vinegar, and salt.

3. Pour in the water plus 1 cup of the tamarind-soaking water and stir. Cook over medium heat, covered, for 30 minutes, until the ingredients are softened. Add more water if needed.

4. Once the ingredients are soft, transfer the cooked mixture to a blender and blend, pulsing for 3 to 5 minutes until it becomes a thick sauce. (A high-speed blender works best here.)

5. Pour the chamoy sauce back into the pot and add the Tajin and lime juice. Stir for 1 minute until the sauce comes together. Taste and add more Tajin and salt as necessary.

**TIP:** Store the chamoy in mason jars or another airtight container in the refrigerator for up to 1 month.

# TAQUERO-STYLE NON-AVOCADO GUACAMOLE SALSA

## *Guacamole Estilo Taquería Sin Aguacate*

The taquero-style sauce is perfect for tacos dorados, for tacos with grilled meats, and used as a dipping sauce. Some call it fake guacamole because no avocados are involved in the preparation. However, it tastes like spicy guacamole salsa, and it is creamy green—a good option when avocados are scarce or when looking into budget-friendly garnishes and sides. And nobody will know it has zucchini because you can't even taste it!

6 cups cold water

6 tomatillos, husked and rinsed

1 medium zucchini, ends removed and cut into large chunks

¼ cup corn oil

½ small white onion, coarsely chopped

2 serrano peppers or jalapeños, stemmed

½ cup fresh cilantro with stems

2 garlic cloves, peeled

1 tablespoon salt

1. In a large pot, cook the water, tomatillos, and zucchini chunks for 5 minutes over medium heat. Remove from the heat and keep it covered.

2. In a large sauté pan or skillet, heat the oil over medium to high heat until shimmering. Fry the onion, serrano peppers, and garlic for 5 to 7 minutes until golden brown. Stir and turn occasionally.

3. Transfer the cooked tomatillos, zucchini, onion, cilantro, serranos, garlic, the oil used for frying, and salt to a blender.

4. Blend on high for 2 to 3 minutes until the sauce emulsifies and becomes a thick sauce mimicking guacamole.

**TIP:** Pour the sauce into a mason jar and store in the refrigerator for up to 5 days. Unlike guacamole, it won't turn brown.

# STREET TACO SALSA
## *Salsa Taquera*

Street Taco Salsa became famous in taco stands and taquerías; that is why many have named it "salsa taquera." The main characteristic is that this sauce has a reddish-orange color and is extra spicy due to the delightful smoky taste of chiles de árbol.

¼ cup corn oil

3 to 6 chiles de árbol, stemmed

¼ white onion, coarsely chopped

2 garlic cloves, peeled

4 Roma tomatoes, halved

1 tablespoon chicken bouillon powder

½ teaspoon coarse salt

⅓ red onion, finely chopped

½ cup coarsely chopped fresh cilantro leaves

1. In a large sauté pan or skillet, heat the oil over medium to high heat until shimmering. Fry the chiles de árbol for 1 to 2 minutes, turning constantly. Remove them from the oil and set aside.

2. Add the onion to the skillet and fry for 3 minutes, sporadically turning. Add the garlic cloves and fry for 2 minutes on both sides until browned.

3. Add the tomatoes and sauté for 3 to 4 minutes, until soft. Season with the chicken bouillon and salt and stir. Simmer for another 2 minutes until the vegetables are soft.

4. Transfer the cooked vegetables, including the oil used for sautéing, to a blender, and blend for 2 to 3 minutes until the sauce emulsifies and changes to a reddish-orange color. It should be a smooth consistency.

5. Pour the sauce into a bowl, stir in the chopped red onion, and top with fresh cilantro before serving. Store in a mason jar in the refrigerator for up to 5 days.

**TIP:** If you prefer a spicier salsa, add more chiles de árbol. Add 2 to 3 tomatillos to the mix and sauté with the tomatoes for tartness. This salsa is perfect for grilled meats and Beef Asada Tacos (page 71).

# DRUNKEN SALSA
## *Salsa Borracha*

The name of Salsa Borracha (drunken sauce) was given because the original recipe has pulque (an alcoholic beverage made of fermented agave nectar) and beer as the main ingredients. However, pulque is a challenging ingredient to find. It can be replaced with mezcal and made Oaxacan style. The mezcal provides additional smoky notes and a delightful bite.

½ medium white onion

2 garlic cloves, peeled

6 pasilla peppers, stemmed

1 ancho pepper, stemmed and seeded

1 cup freshly squeezed orange juice

3 tablespoons mezcal or tequila reposado

1 tablespoon salt

¼ cup crumbled queso cotija or queso añejo (aged Mexican cheese), for serving

1. Heat a large nonstick skillet or cast-iron comal over high heat and toast the onion and garlic cloves for 2 minutes, occasionally turning. When they are toasted, remove from the heat and set them aside.

2. Turn off the heat and toast the pasilla and ancho peppers for 1 minute on each side in the same comal. Turn several times to avoid burning.

3. In a medium saucepan, combine the orange juice, roasted veggies, and peppers. Cook over medium heat for 15 minutes until the peppers are softened.

4. Transfer this mixture to a blender and add the mezcal and salt. Blend for 2 to 3 minutes until smooth.

5. Pour the sauce into a bowl and garnish with the crumbled queso cotija. Store the salsa in a mason jar in the refrigerator for up to 4 days.

**TIP:** Pasilla pepper is called *chile negro* (black pepper). It is available in stores that carry Hispanic products and on Amazon. Salsa borracha is perfect for Lamb Barbacoa Tacos (page 84) and Beer Veal Cutlets Tacos (page 76).

# PINTO BEANS TWO WAYS
## *Frijoles Pintos de Olla y Refritos*

*Frijoles de Olla* (pot beans) are named as such because the traditional way of cooking them was inside a clay pot over a wood fire, and for two hours or more. Nowadays, the best way to cook beans is to use an electric pressure cooker (I use a six-quart Instant Pot).

### FOR THE PINTO BEANS

1 tablespoon corn oil or pork lard
½ medium white onion
3 garlic cloves, peeled
1 chile de árbol, stemmed
   and seeded
1 tablespoon ground cumin
1 teaspoon dried
   Mexican oregano
1 pound dried pinto beans, rinsed
6 to 8 cups water
1 tablespoon salt

### FOR THE REFRIED PINTO BEANS

1 tablespoon pork lard, bacon fat,
   or corn oil
½ cup crumbled queso fresco

### TO MAKE THE PINTO BEANS

1. Pour the oil into an Instant Pot and select the Sauté mode. Quick-fry the onion and garlic for 2 minutes, until browned. Add the chile de árbol, cumin, and oregano. Stir and sauté for 1 minute, until fragrant.

2. Add the pinto beans to the pot and mix with the sautéed ingredients. Add the water and fill to right below the line marked with ½.

3. Close the lid and cook on high pressure for 30 to 45 minutes. When cooking is complete, allow the pressure to release naturally. Carefully open the lid.

4. Season the beans with salt. Separate 2 cups for making refried beans (see steps 5 to 7). Pour the rest of the beans into airtight containers and refrigerate for up to 5 days or freeze for 6 months.

### TO MAKE THE REFRIED PINTO BEANS

5. Place 2 cups of cooked, warm pinto beans in a blender, and blend on high for 3 minutes until smooth.

6. In a medium sauté pan or skillet, heat the pork lard over medium heat until melted. Pour in the beans and fry for 5 to 7 minutes, constantly stirring. When you see the bottom of the pan, the beans are ready.

7. Serve garnished with crumbled queso fresco.

# HOMEMADE FLOUR TORTILLAS
## *Tortillas de Harina Caseras*

Flour tortillas are a staple in Northern Mexican cuisine. Depending on the area, tortillas could be thick and small, thin and medium size, and extra large called *sobaqueras o de agua* (water-based tortillas). Every evening, tortillas are freshly made in many Mexican homes to pair with homestyle classics and for tacos.

2 cups all-purpose flour, sifted
1 teaspoon salt
1 teaspoon baking powder
½ cup vegetable shortening, at
  room temperature
1 cup hot water

**TIP:** Using the correct measurements, resting the dough, keeping it moist and covered, and using a thick cast-iron skillet will produce the best results.

1. In a medium bowl, combine the flour, salt, and baking powder and mix well. Using your hands, incorporate the shortening until the texture is sandy.

2. Add the water a little bit at a time, and knead the dough for 5 to 8 minutes, until moist and soft but not sticky.

3. Form the dough into a ball, cover it with plastic wrap, place it in a container with a lid, and let it rest for 1 hour.

4. Divide the dough into 12 balls. Cover the balls with a cloth to prevent them from drying out.

5. Sprinkle some flour on a work surface and using a floured rolling pin, roll one dough ball into a thick 8-inch circle. Flip and turn the dough to achieve the rounded form. Repeat the process with the remaining dough balls.

6. Preheat a large cast-iron skillet over medium heat. Working one at a time, cook the tortilla for 30 seconds. When bubbles form, flip the tortilla and press it with a press or a double-folded thick towel.

7. The tortilla will start puffing. When golden-brown spots are visible on both sides, the tortilla is ready. Wrap the tortillas in a tea towel and repeat with the remaining dough.

# HABANERO RED ONION SALSA
## *Salsa de Habanero Estilo Xnipec*

The name *xnipec* is Mayan and means wet dog's nose, because this salsa is so hot that it makes your nose sweat. This salsa is perfect for tacos and other fried small bites such as nachos, quesadillas, tostadas, and taquitos dorados. I like it with Yucatecan-inspired food such as Yucatán Fish Tacos (page 55) and grilled seafood and meats. But it is the perfect garnish for soups and seafood cocktails.

¼ cup freshly squeezed orange juice

Juice of 1 lime

1 teaspoon coarse salt

3 Roma tomatoes, diced

1 small red onion, chopped

½ cup coarsely chopped fresh cilantro

2 habaneros, seeded and chopped

1. In a large bowl, combine the orange juice, lime juice, and salt. Stir for 2 minutes to dissolve the salt.

2. Add the tomatoes, onion, cilantro, and habaneros, and mix well.

3. Set it aside to marinate for 30 minutes. Serve in a bowl, or store in a mason jar in the refrigerator for up to 2 days.

**TIP:** Use food-safe rubber gloves to avoid burning your hands while handling the habanero peppers. Use fewer habaneros and remove the vein for a milder taste. Green habaneros tend to be less spicy than red and orange habaneros.

**TRIVIA:** Many of the world's favorite taco fillings were originally grown and eaten by the indigenous civilizations of Mexico, including avocados, chiles, corn, and tomatoes.

## CHAPTER 7

# DRINKS AND DESSERTS

< Mango Mezcal Mojito, page 106

# MANGO MEZCAL MOJITO
## *Mojito de Mango con Mezcal*

Did you know that mezcal is the same as tequila? The difference between the two is that mezcal is made in Oaxaca using thirty varieties of agave, and it is cooked in a pit with lava rocks, firewood, and charcoal giving it a smoky flavor. Tequila is made only with blue agave, it is steamed, and it has a denomination of origin, meaning that Tequila, Jalisco, is the only place approved to use the name "tequila." Young mezcal, such as Espadín, is typically used for mixed cocktails as it is smoother and pairs well with different combinations and fruit juices. The smoky notes go nicely with mango, making this Mango Mezcal Mojito a delight.

¼ cup chopped fresh mango
Juice of 1 lime
1 tablespoon sugar
6 fresh mint leaves
2 ounces mezcal espadín
Sparkling water, chilled

1. In a tall glass, combine the mango, lime juice, sugar, and mint leaves.

2. Using a cocktail muddler or fork, lightly mash the mango and mint leaves into the sugar and lime juice.

3. Fill the glass with ice. Pour in the mezcal and top off with sparkling water.

**TIP:** Summer is my favorite time of the year to enjoy a refreshing mojito because of the wide variety of fruits in season. Switch up the flavor of your mojito by substituting fresh strawberries, raspberries, or nectarines for the mango.

**TRIVIA:** There are many theories about the exact origin of the mojito, but it was originally made in Cuba and features light rum, mint, sugar, and soda water.

# THE HIDALGO
## *El Hidalgo*

This drink isn't traditional, but it highlights tequila blanco in an unconventional and tasty way. It features a real kick of both flavor and heat with the addition of jalapeño simple syrup. Serve on the rocks in an old-fashioned glass.

**FOR THE JALAPEÑO SIMPLE SYRUP**

1 cup sugar

1 cup water

2 jalapeños, sliced

**FOR THE DRINK**

Lime wedge, for rimming glass

Salt, for rimming glass

2 ounces tequila blanco

½ ounce orange liqueur

½ ounce jalapeño simple syrup

¾ ounce freshly squeezed lime juice

Jalapeño slice, seeded, for garnish

**TO MAKE THE JALAPEÑO SIMPLE SYRUP**

1. In a small saucepan, combine the sugar and water and boil until dissolved. Remove from the heat.

2. Add the jalapeños to the syrup mixture to steep for at least 20 minutes. Strain and chill for use.

**TO MAKE THE DRINK**

3. Slice a lime wedge perpendicularly, and then slide the flesh along the rim of the glass. Dip the glass upside down into a dish of salt.

4. Carefully fill the glass with ice cubes. Pour in the tequila, orange liqueur, and jalapeño simple syrup. Mix gently. Squeeze a full quarter of a lime into the drink and stir again (lime can be discarded or dropped in the glass).

5. Top with a jalapeño slice or use it to garnish the rim and serve.

**TIP:** Use store-bought jalapeño simple syrup. The best tequila for this drink is silver tequila blanco.

# PIÑA COLADA AGUA FRESCA
## *Agua Fresca de Piña Colada*

This Piña Colada Agua Fresca is a family-friendly version inspired by the classic cocktail with fresh pineapple and shredded coconut. This beverage is so creamy and delicious you won't even notice that there isn't any alcohol. (Although you can always add a shot of rum to your glass before serving.) The cream of coconut adds more coconut flavor and sweetness and a creamy consistency for a dreamy, tropical delight.

6 to 8 cups water, divided
2 cups fresh pineapple chunks
1 cup shredded coconut
1 cup coconut cream
Sugar (optional)
Maraschino cherries (optional)

1. Place 4 cups of water, pineapple, and coconut in a blender and process until smooth.

2. Strain the puree into a 2-quart pitcher. Stir in the coconut cream and enough water to fill the pitcher.

3. Sweeten with sugar (if using).

4. Refrigerate until ready to serve. Serve in glasses filled with ice.

5. Garnish each with a maraschino cherry (if using).

**TIP:** Enjoy this tropical agua fresca even in the winter by using 1 (15.5-ounce) can or a frozen bag of pineapple chunks, instead of the fresh. Replace the shredded coconut with coconut ice cream.

# MANGO-LIME AGUA FRESCA
## *Agua Fresca de Mango Limón*

Aguas frescas are made with a combination of fruit, seeds, flowers, and grains, which are then blended with water and sugar. In Mexico, street vendors commonly sell them, but drinking refreshing fruity drinks started at home to use up leftover fruit. Aguas frescas are a delicious thirst quencher after a day in the sun or to pair with a meal.

1 large mango, peeled, pitted, and cut into chunks
1½ cups cold water
Juice of 2 limes
2 teaspoons agave syrup or sugar
1 lime, cut into thin slices, for garnishing

1. In a blender, puree the mango and water until smooth.

2. Press the puree through a strainer or fine-mesh sieve into two glasses filled with ice. Stir in the lime juice and agave syrup.

3. Garnish with the lime slices and serve immediately.

**TIP:** Use canned or frozen mangos instead of fresh ones. Make the agua fresca a day in advance, chill it in the refrigerator, minus any ice. Make the drink bubbly by adding a splash of mineral water or add an ounce of tequila for an adult beverage.

# OATMEAL HORCHATA
*Horchata de Avena*

Rice and cinnamon horchata is among the most popular flavors for Mexican aguas frescas. However, oats and barley are common ingredients for making horchata drinks, too. This milky drink is part of the Spanish heritage inspired by the *horchata de chufas*, a summery drink typical of Valencia, Spain, brought by the nuns to the New World.

6 cups water

1 cup old-fashioned oats or oat flour

1 cinnamon stick

1 (14-ounce) can sweetened condensed milk

Sugar (optional)

Ground cinnamon, for serving (optional)

1. Place the water, oats, and cinnamon stick in a blender and process until smooth. Strain the puree into a 2-quart pitcher.

2. Add the sweetened condensed milk and stir until it dissolves completely. Add the sugar (if using).

3. Refrigerate until ready to serve. Pour into tall glasses filled with ice and sprinkle with cinnamon powder (if using).

**TIP:** Turn this into a grown-up treat by adding a shot of rum to each glass before serving.

# MEXICAN HOT CHOCOLATE
## *Champurrado*

Champurrado is traditional Mexican atole (a warm beverage thickened with masa) flavored with chocolate and thickened with masa harina. Think of it as a thicker cinnamon-spiced hot cocoa with a slightly grainy texture. The origin of this drink is pre-Hispanic, dating from the time of the Aztecs. The difference between atole and champurrado is that the latter is made with cornstarch. Nowadays, Mexican chocolate is readily available in supermarkets and often found with other hot chocolate offerings in the same aisle. Just look for a yellow and red hexagon-shaped box.

3 cups whole milk, divided

½ cup masa harina

3 cups water

1 (3-ounce) tablet Mexican chocolate, cut into wedges

1 (3-inch) cinnamon stick

3 tablespoons sugar

1. Place 1 cup of the milk and the masa harina in a blender and process until smooth. Set it aside.

2. In a medium saucepan, heat the remaining 2 cups of milk, the water, the chocolate, and the cinnamon stick over medium heat, stirring occasionally, for 8 to 10 minutes, until the chocolate has completely melted. Remove the cinnamon stick.

3. Stir in the masa harina mixture and the sugar. Stirring constantly with a wire whisk to prevent lumps from forming, continue simmering for 12 to 15 minutes until the champurrado thickens. Remove from the heat and serve hot.

**TIP:** Substitute the Mexican chocolate with ¼ cup of cocoa powder, 1½ teaspoons of ground cinnamon, and 2 tablespoons of sugar. For making chocolate atole, substitute the masa harina with cornstarch.

# CHAMOY MICHELADA
## *Chamochela–Michelada de Chamoy*

Chamochela is a new take on a Mexican michelada, but this one has chamoy for a sweet, sour, and spicy touch. Classic micheladas only have lime juice, Worcestershire sauce, Tabasco, ice, and beer. But bartenders in Mexico have started creating new versions, and the chamoy flavor is popular. This recipe uses homemade Tamarind Sauce "Chamoy" (page 96), giving a better taste and no added chemicals or unnecessary food colorings.

1 lime, halved plus juice
  of 3 limes

2 tablespoons chamoy powder
  or Tajin

1 cup tomato juice or clamato

4 teaspoons Tamarind Sauce
  "Chamoy" (page 96)

1 cup crushed ice

1 (12-ounce) bottle light or dark
  Mexican beer, chilled

2 tamarind candy sticks
  (optional)

1. Use half a lime and wet the rim of two tall glasses with the lime juice. Place 2 tablespoons of the chamoy powder on a small plate. Dip the glasses in this spicy salt and set them aside.

2. In a large pitcher, combine the tomato juice, lime juice, and the chamoy sauce and mix with a long spoon for 15 seconds.

3. Put the crushed ice in the prepared glasses. Pour the tomato mix to fill half the glass with this mix.

4. Fill the remainder of the glass with the chilled beer and garnish it with a tamarind candy stick (if using).

**TIP:** As an option, garnish the drink with mango and orange slices dusted with Tajin spicy salt instead of using a tamarind candy stick.

# MEXICAN RICE PUDDING
## *Arroz con Leche*

Rice pudding originated in Asia, and from there was adopted by Europe. After the sixteenth century, it came to Latin America. My grandfather was a refugee from Spain, and my grandmother used to make Asturias-style rice pudding with anisette, as that was the style he enjoyed most. Each household in Mexico has its family recipe. My mom loved adding orange peel, so I do the same.

1 cup long- or short-grain rice

1 cup water

Peel of 1 orange

1 tablespoon ground cinnamon, plus a pinch for serving

1 cinnamon stick

Pinch coarse salt

1 (12-ounce) can evaporated milk

1 cup whole milk

1 tablespoon vanilla extract

1 (14-ounce) can condensed milk

1. In a soup pot or cast-iron Dutch oven, combine the rice, water, orange peel, cinnamon, cinnamon stick, and salt over medium heat. Cook for 10 minutes, stirring with a wooden spoon.

2. After the first boil, the rice will become creamy. Add the evaporated milk, milk, and vanilla and continue to cook, stirring, for another 20 minutes.

3. Add the condensed milk and stir again when the rice is soft to the touch. Cook for another 10 to 15 minutes, until creamy.

4. Remove and discard the orange peel and cinnamon stick. Turn off the heat and cover the pot with the lid.

5. Serve warm or cold, sprinkled with a bit of ground cinnamon.

**TIP:** Short-grain rice makes the rice pudding sticky, so use that type of rice if you prefer that texture. Serve the rice with fresh fruit or pour it in a ice-pop mold and put it in the freezer to make ice pops.

# CINNAMON BUÑUELOS
## *Buñuelos de Canela*

The buñuelos are another delight brought from the Old World to the New. Some say the recipe originated in the north of Spain. These fried treats are typical for the holidays in Mexico and are sold in street fairs. The traditional technique for forming the buñuelos is sitting down, placing the dough on the knee, and stretching it to create a paper-thin tortilla. But buñuelos cannot be confused with flour tortillas, as the dough has different ingredients.

1 cup all-purpose flour

3 cups plus ½ tablespoon sugar, divided

½ teaspoon salt

½ teaspoon baking powder

½ cup water

1 tablespoon corn oil or melted unsalted butter

2 cups corn oil, for frying

3 tablespoons ground cinnamon

1. In a mixing bowl, combine the flour, ½ tablespoon sugar, the salt, and the baking powder and whisk. Then add the water and oil and mix to make the dough.

2. Transfer the dough to a clean surface and knead for 15 minutes until it doesn't stick to your fingers.

3. Divide the dough into 12 portions. Make dough balls with your hands and keep them covered with a cloth to keep the dough from drying.

4. Take one portion of the dough, sprinkle some flour to the surface, and form a superthin 6- to 8-inch round with a rolling pin.

5. In a large, deep sauté pan or skillet, heat the oil over medium-high heat. Fry each buñuelo for 1 to 2 minutes per side until golden and crisp. Transfer the buñuelos to a paper-towel-lined plate to remove excess oil.

6. On a large plate, mix the remaining 3 cups of sugar with the cinnamon. Dip the warm buñuelos in the cinnamon mixture on both sides.

**TIP:** For crispier buñuelos, make a tea with clean tomatillo husks and use it instead of water.

# COCONUT FLAN
## *Flan de Coco*

The word *flan* is the French equivalent of the Latin word *fladon*, which means flat cake. Spaniards brought the flan to Mexico, where flan is one of the top desserts of choice. I love this version with toasted coconut.

Nonstick cooking spray

6 tablespoons dulce de leche syrup

1 (14-ounce) can sweetened condensed milk

1 (12-ounce) can Thai-style evaporated coconut milk

4 large eggs, at room temperature

1 tablespoon vanilla extract

1 teaspoon coconut extract

¼ cup toasted coconut flakes

1. Preheat the oven to 350°F.

2. Spray an 8-cup Bundt pan with nonstick cooking spray and coat the bottom of the pan with dulce de leche syrup. Fill a large baking pan that the Bundt pan will fit inside of halfway with water and set aside.

3. Place the condensed milk, coconut milk, eggs, vanilla, and coconut extract in a blender. Blend on high for 2 minutes, and pour the flan mix into the Bundt pan.

4. Cover the Bundt pan with foil and place it inside the water bath. Bake the flan for 1 hour and 30 minutes, or until it's lightly colored and firm to the touch (but not solid).

5. Remove the baking pan from the oven and the flan from the warm water bath. Cool it at room temperature for 1 hour, covered. Refrigerate it for 24 hours before serving.

6. To unmold the flan, turn the Bundt pan onto a platter. Pull off the pan slowly. The flan will plop. Add more dulce de leche syrup if needed.

7. To decorate, sprinkle with the toasted coconut flakes. Cut and serve.

**TIP:** If using a mixer or whisking the flan mixture by hand, strain it before pouring it into the Bundt pan. Flan requires a double boiler to avoid overcooking.

# STRAWBERRY ICE POPS
## *Paletas Heladas de Fresa*

The tradition of fruit *paletas* in Mexico started in Michoacán in the 1940s. Now, this tradition has surpassed frontiers, and you can find famous La Michoacana ice pops all over the United States. Although these ice pops are delicious, making them fresh at home is a great idea. I cannot think of a better summer dessert than an ice pop—especially a Mexican ice pop that's loaded with fruit. Once you make this version, be inspired to try countless others—the sky is the limit, depending on your creativity.

1 pint fresh strawberries, stemmed

½ cup sugar

½ cup freshly squeezed lime juice

1½ teaspoons finely grated lime zest

1. In a blender, puree the strawberries, sugar, lime juice, and lime zest.

2. Pour the mixture into ice-pop molds. Cover and insert ice-pop sticks.

3. Transfer to the freezer to freeze until solid, at least 8 hours.

4. To release the pops from the molds, quickly dip them in hot water or use a mold that allows for a quick release. Serve immediately.

**TIP:** For best results, freeze the ice pops overnight. Follow the same recipe and use other seasonal fruits such as raspberries, mango, blackberries, watermelon, and honeydew.

# CLASSIC LIME MARGARITA
## *Margarita Clásica*

The cocktail margarita is famous and legendary. The story says this cocktail is named after a woman that inspired the drink and was created by a bartender in Tijuana. But there are many stories about the origin. Whoever made the drink, I think, was genius because who doesn't enjoy a refreshing margarita?

**FOR THE TEQUILA MARGARITA**
½ lime
2 tablespoons salt, for rimming
½ cup ice
½ cup tequila blanco
½ cup freshly squeezed lime juice
¼ cup orange liqueur
2 tablespoons sugar
1 lime, cut into thin slices, for decorating

**FOR THE MEZCAL MARGARITA**
½ lime
2 tablespoons smoked spicy worm salt for rimming
½ cup ice
½ cup mezcal espadín
½ cup freshly squeezed orange juice
½ cup freshly squeezed lime juice
2 tablespoons sugar
1 lime, cut into thin slices for decorating

**TO MAKE THE TEQUILA MARGARITA**

1. Use half a lime to wet the rim of the glass with lime juice. Place the salt on a plate and dip the glass upside down in the salt. Remove and set aside.

2. Place the ice, tequila, lime juice, orange liqueur, and sugar in a blender. Blend for 2 minutes on high.

3. Pour the margarita mix into the salted glass and garnish with a lime slice.

**TO MAKE THE MEZCAL MARGARITA (MEZCALITA)**

1. Use half a lime to wet the rim of the glass with lime juice. Place the salt on a plate and dip the glass upside down in it. Remove and set aside.

2. Add the ice, mezcal, orange juice, lime juice, and sugar to the blender. Blend for 2 minutes on high.

3. Pour the mezcal mix into the salted glass and garnish with a lime slice.

**TIP:** Explore other combinations with mango or strawberries, or if you prefer, place the ice in the glass and shake the ingredients in a cocktail shaker to serve the margarita on the rocks.

# MOSAIC GELATIN
## *Gelatina Mosaico*

One of the favorite desserts in Mexico is Mosaic Gelatin. It has that name because the gelatin has different colors, simulating a mosaic or stained glass.

**FOR THE MOSAIC GELATIN**

1 (3-ounce) box strawberry-flavored gelatin

1 (3-ounce) box lemon-flavored gelatin

1 (3-ounce) box pineapple-flavored gelatin

3 cups boiling water, divided

3 cups cold water, divided

Nonstick cooking spray

**FOR THE MILK GELATIN**

2 (¼-ounce) packets unflavored gelatin

½ cup water, at room temperature

1 cup warm water

1 (12-ounce) can condensed milk

1 teaspoon vanilla extract

Nonstick cooking spray

**TO MAKE THE GELATIN**

1. In three separate medium bowls, dissolve each gelatin flavor with 1 cup of boiling water. Whisk for 2 minutes until the white bubbles disappear. Add 1 cup of cold water to each and whisk again.

2. Spray 3 (2-cup) rectangular Pyrex pans with vegetable oil and pour in the gelatin.

3. Refrigerate for 3 to 6 hours until firm.

4. Cut the gelatin into squares using a sharp knife.

5. Drop the squares in a bowl, mix the colors, and set aside.

**TO MAKE THE MILK GELATIN**

6. In a small bowl, dissolve the gelatin with the room-temperature water. Let the gelatin bloom for 2 minutes, then cook in the microwave for 1 minute, until the gelatin dissolves.

7. Place 1 cup of warm water, the dissolved gelatin, the condensed milk, and the vanilla in the blender and blend on high for 2 minutes.

## TO MAKE THE MOSAIC GELATIN

8. Spray a 10-cup Bundt pan with cooking spray.

9. Add the mixed flavored gelatin squares and space evenly.

10. Pour the milk gelatin slowly, covering the gelatin squares, and refrigerate overnight.

11. To unmold, press the edges with your fingers. Sprinkle about 1 teaspoon of water on a platter, turn the Bundt pan onto the platter, shake, and pull off the pan slowly.

. . . . . . . . . . . . . . . . . . . . . . . . . . . . . . . . . . . . . . . . . . . .

**TIP:** Use any gelatin flavors or colors of your choice.

. . . . . . . . . . . . . . . . . . . . . . . . . . . . . . . . . . . . . . . . . . . .

# CINNAMON CHURROS
## *Churros de Canela*

Churros originated in Catalonia, Spain, and were brought to Mexico during the colonization. Some say churros began in China as a breakfast item and were brought to Spain by the Portuguese. Churros are made with a simple wheat dough, fried, and sprinkled with cinnamon and sugar. They're popular during the winter, served with hot chocolate as an evening snack.

½ cup whole milk
½ cup water
1 cup plus 1 tablespoon sugar, divided
¼ teaspoon salt
2 tablespoons unsalted butter
1 cup flour, sifted
2 large eggs, beaten
3 cups canola or corn oil (not peanut)
1 teaspoon ground cinnamon

1. In a large soup pot, combine the milk, the water, 1 tablespoon of sugar, and the salt over medium heat and whisk for 5 to 7 minutes. Add the butter and continue whisking until melted.

2. Turn off the heat and add the flour, a little bit at a time, whisking vigorously until integrated. Add the eggs and whisk again for about 15 minutes until the dough turns soft and silky. Transfer the dough to a piping bag with a star tip.

3. In a large, deep sauté pan or skillet, heat the oil to between 350°F and 360°F. (If not using a thermometer, drop some dough in the oil; if it starts bubbling and browning rapidly, the oil is ready.)

4. You can make straight lines of dough, rounds, or twists. Fry the churros for 3 to 5 minutes until golden brown. Use tongs to transfer the churros to a paper-towel-lined plate to remove the excess oil.

5. On another plate, mix the remaining 1 cup of sugar and the cinnamon. While the churros are still warm, dredge them in the cinnamon mixture and serve.

**TIP:** Add a side of caramel or chocolate sauce for dipping.

Mexican Hot Chocolate (Page 111), Cinnamon Churros (Page 120) >

# MEASUREMENT CONVERSIONS

**OVEN TEMPERATURES**

| FAHRENHEIT | CELSIUS (APPROXIMATE) |
|---|---|
| 250°F | 120°C |
| 300°F | 150°C |
| 325°F | 165°C |
| 350°F | 180°C |
| 375°F | 190°C |
| 400°F | 200°C |
| 425°F | 220°C |
| 450°F | 230°C |

**WEIGHT EQUIVALENTS**

| U.S. STANDARD | METRIC (APPROXIMATE) |
|---|---|
| ½ ounce | 15 g |
| 1 ounce | 30 g |
| 2 ounces | 60 g |
| 4 ounces | 115 g |
| 8 ounces | 225 g |
| 12 ounces | 340 g |
| 16 ounces or 1 pound | 455 g |

**VOLUME EQUIVALENTS**

|  | U.S. STANDARD | U.S. STANDARD (OUNCES) | METRIC (APPROXIMATE) |
|---|---|---|---|
| LIQUID | 2 tablespoons | 1 fl. oz. | 30 mL |
|  | ¼ cup | 2 fl. oz. | 60 mL |
|  | ½ cup | 4 fl. oz. | 120 mL |
|  | 1 cup | 8 fl. oz. | 240 mL |
|  | 1½ cups | 12 fl. oz. | 355 mL |
|  | 2 cups or 1 pint | 16 fl. oz. | 475 mL |
|  | 4 cups or 1 quart | 32 fl. oz. | 1 L |
|  | 1 gallon | 128 fl. oz. | 4 L |
| DRY | ⅛ teaspoon | – | 0.5 mL |
|  | ¼ teaspoon | – | 1 mL |
|  | ½ teaspoon | – | 2 mL |
|  | ¾ teaspoon | – | 4 mL |
|  | 1 teaspoon | – | 5 mL |
|  | 1 tablespoon | – | 15 mL |
|  | ¼ cup | – | 59 mL |
|  | ⅓ cup | – | 79 mL |
|  | ½ cup | – | 118 mL |
|  | ⅔ cup | – | 156 mL |
|  | ¾ cup | – | 177 mL |
|  | 1 cup | – | 235 mL |
|  | 2 cups or 1 pint | – | 475 mL |
|  | 3 cups | – | 700 mL |
|  | 4 cups or 1 quart | – | 1 L |
|  | ½ gallon | – | 2 L |
|  | 1 gallon | – | 4 L |

# REFERENCES

The Austin Eater. austin.eater.com/2016/2/19/11060078/breakfast-taco-austin-history.

Chapa, Martha. *Los tacos de Mexico (Mexican Tacos)*. Editorial Ink, 2013. Kindle Edition.

Gourmet de Mexico. "Conoce el origen del coctel Margarita." Accessed February 10, 2022 gourmetdemexico.com.mx/bebidas/conoce-el-origen-del-coctel-margarita.

Guinness World Records. "Largest Taco." Accessed February 18, 2022. guinnessworldrecords .com/world-records/largest-taco.

Holtz, Deborah, and Juan Carlos Mena. *Tacopedia: The Taco Encyclopedia*. Phaidon Press, 2015.

Jack Trivia. "Tacos & Burritos." Accessed February 18, 2022. jacktrivia.com /tacos-and-burritos.

Larousse Cocina (Larousse Mexican Kitchen). Accessed January 20–February 20, 2022. laroussecocina.mx.

Liquor.com. "6 Things You Should Know About the Mojito." Accessed March 8, 2022. liquor.com/articles/mojito.

Nahuatl Dictionary. Accessed February 1–20, 2022. nahuatl.uoregon.edu.

Prestige Food Trucks. "History of Food Trucks and How They've Shaped America." Accessed February 20, 2022. prestigefoodtrucks.com/2020/03/history -of-food-trucks-and-how-theyve-shaped-america.

Rivas, Heriberto Garcia. *Cocina Prehispánica Mexicana (Mexican Pre-Hispanic Cuisine)*. Panorama Editorial, 2016.

Salt & Wind. "From Mexico con Amor: Foods That Originated in Mexico." Accessed February 20, 2022. saltandwind.com/stories/355-ingredients-foods -historically-from-mexico.

Thrillist. "The Crazy Contentious History of Taco Tuesday." Accessed February 18, 2022. thrillist.com/eat/nation/history-of-taco-tuesday-when-did-it-start.

Torrerosa. "Paloma, el cóctel del mes de junio." Accessed February 10, 2022. torrerosa.com/blog/coctel-mes-paloma-tequila.

Zurita, Ricardo Muñoz. *Larousse Diccionario Enciclopedico de la Cocina Mexicana (Mexican Cuisine Encyclopedia, Spanish version)*. Larousse Mexico, 2013.

# INDEX

## ACKNOWLEDGMENTS

I want to thank my editorial team for their professionalism and dedication while creating this cookbook. Without your help, this third dream book would not have become a reality.

I am thankful to my editor, Sierra Machado, for her patience and support during this new cookbook's writing and research process.

I am grateful for my husband's support during the process. Without your love and patience, I would not have been able to sustain all those long days of recipe testing, sampling, and writing.

And to all of you, Mexican cuisine and taco lovers who have been following my steps, a BIG thank-you! I hope you will find *Taco Obsession Cookbook* helpful and inspiring to cook Mexican tacos at home.

## ABOUT THE AUTHOR

**Adriana Martin** is a home chef and founder of adrianasbestrecipes.com. She is a Latina food writer specializing in recipe development influenced by Mexico's culinary culture and European cuisine. Her grandmother taught her how to cook, and now her mission is to inspire others to make homemade meals.

Adriana teaches online cooking classes, is a trained food stylist and photographer, and has published thousands of recipes online. She is the author of *Best of Mexican Cooking: 75 Authentic Home-Style Recipes for Beginners* and *Super Easy Taco Cookbook*.

LATISM has recognized Adriana as among the Top 100 most influential Latina bloggers, and Telemundo awarded Adriana a TECLA Awards under the category of best food creator.

CPSIA information can be obtained
at www.ICGtesting.com
Printed in the USA
JSHW021759191222
35156JS00007B/189